Explorations
in Freeform Peyote Beading

DESIGNING ORIGINAL ART JEWELRY AND BEYOND

by Karen Williams

Published by Skunk Hill Studio

1020 1st Ave, S. Suite 203, Seattle, WA 98134-1235

For information about desk and examination copies, or other special requests, please contact Karen Williams at skunkhillstudio@gmail.com.

SKUNK HILL STUDIO

Seattle, Washington
www.skunkhillstudio.com, skunkhillstudio@gmail.com
©2014 all rights reserved

Table of Contents

Acknowledgments

They say it takes a village to raise a child. I know it took a global village to birth this book. My heartfelt thanks go out to the wonderful people from around the world who believed in this book enough to back it before the first page was written. This book is truly for you.

Aglarele * Lori Blanchard of Alainn Jewelry * Capitan Holy Hippie * Alisa Siceloff of Armored Mermaid * Amanda M Wacasey * Angela Fazio * Anne Marie Desaulniers of Artful Dreamer * Bev Choy of VChoy Jewelry Designs * Bobbie Rafferty * Bonita Kroon * Carla J Mazzone * Caroline G Heck * Carrie Johnson * Chris Simmons * Connie S Gordon * Cortney Phillips of Baubles by Cortney * Crystal Ludlow * Cindy Hambrick, Pootie Beads * Cynthia Machata from Antiquity Travelers * Diana Lee Hofmann * Dixie Polakoff * Elizabeth Gillespie * F. Cockwill * Francie Broadie * Glen Lawrence * Jan Tharaldson * Janice Sullivan * Jean Hutter * Jeffrey Chou (aka Mal, my one-time twin) * Jennifer Porter * Becca Hay * Judith Deshaies * JJ Jacobs - Coming Abstractions * Judy Pennington * Julie Schmidt Bowen of AutEvDesigns * Julie Riecher Vasquez * Karin Slaton, Backstory Beads * Kathleen Standard * Kim Dworak * KJ of KJ's Beadacious Beads * Leah Kaufman & Nathan Clarenburg * Leanne Kirsch * Lisa Jones * Liz Hart of TreeTop Beadworks * Liz White * Lois Athena Buhalis * Lori Finney * Lynn Appleget * Mandi Ainsworth * Margaret M. St. John * Margaret Rehnstrom * Margo Lynn Hablutzel * Marlene Emmons of From ME To You * Melody Anne Martin * Michele Soncrant * Michael Randall * Nada Djordjevic * Nancy Dale * Natalia Malysheva * Alyxx S Berg * Patty Flowers * Patricia Richey of Riverpoint Studio * Robin Coventry * Roxanne Moore * Ruth Duck * Sally Russick * Sarah Sequins * Sheron Buchele Rowland * Shirley Moore * Sophia Owens * Stacy Lynne Hotes * Susan Kirby of SBK Designs * Tamera Mickelson * Tammy Bowman * Tanya Goodwin * Tilinka of Perilous Puppets * Tina Clark of Cairngorm Designs * Tres Henry * Vala Richmond * Veralynne Malone of Vera Designs * Yvette Benjamin

I also want to send a very special thank you to Lori Finney, Bonita Kroon, Mary Gross, Sarah Meadows, Jennifer Porter and Mary Foyes. Thank you for taking the time to comb through the book's revisions and for your detailed feedback; your assistance was priceless. All remaining errors are mine alone.

CHAPTER ONE

Getting Started

Basic Peyote Stitch

String a stop bead leaving a 6-8 inch tail. The stop bead temporarily holds everything in place while you start stitching. Remove the stop bead after 4-5 rows of stitching. Weave the thread tail into your work.

Even Count Peyote (Rows 1-3)

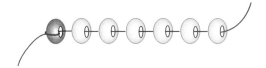

1) String a line of beads. This is your starting row.

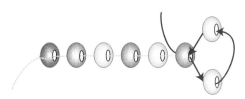

2) Pick up one more bead. Stitch back through the second bead in your starting row. (The alternating bead colors in the diagram are for illustrative purposes only).

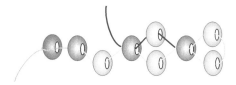

3 & 4) Continue back along your starting row. Pick up one bead at a time and stitch through every second bead.

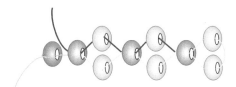

Ready to start Row Four.

An understanding of the variations of the basic peyote stitch is essential before starting on any freeform peyote project. Traditional peyote stitch patterns are designed for either even or odd counts. With freeform peyote, the **bead count changes dynamically** as you work with different sizes of beads. Freeform peyote is easier if you are comfortable switching back and forth, or better yet, forgetting about even and odd counts all together and simply working with what you have.

Before we really get started, here's a quick review.

1) **With peyote stitch**, you always begin by stringing a line of beads. It helps to use a stop bead to hold everything in place as you get started. Whether you work with odd or even count peyote simply depends upon the number of beads you string. When counting the beads in your starting row, do not count your stop bead!

Once you've strung your starting line, you are ready to begin the first real row of peyote stitch.

2) **Pick up one more bead.** Reversing direction, stitch back through the second to last bead from your initial string. Pull everything tight so that the two beads on the end sit side by side. (The beading always looks a little like a dragonfly body with eyes to me at this point).

3) **Pick up another bead.** Skipping a bead, stitch through the next bead back along your starting length.

4) **Keep working your peyote stitch,** picking up one bead at a time and stitching through every other bead until you reach the far end of your starting length.

Ready for Row 4. This is where things go differently for odd and even count peyote. The following page shares stitch diagrams for both.

Even & Odd Count Peyote Stitch

Even Count Peyote: Row 4 & Beyond

Starting Row 4. Pick up one bead then reverse stitching directions. Stitch back through the last bead you just added.

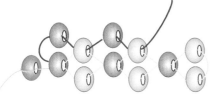

Continue stitching along the length, adding one bead at a time. Stitch through the beads added in the previous row.

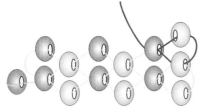

Row Five. When you reach the end of Row Four, pick up one bead and reverse directions again.

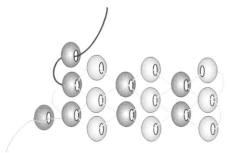

Continue building the rows like setting bricks in a wall. Each row is a half step up from the one before. The rows also remind me of teeth in a zipper.

Odd Count Peyote

Stitch counts can change dramatically from row to row when working with different sizes and shapes of beads. It's useful to have several methods of dealing with the occasional odd count row. Here are three suggestions:

Method 1: Odd Count Peyote

Pick up the last bead, stitch back through three beads from Row 1 as shown in diagram. Reverse directions and stitch back to the starting end, coming out of first bead from Row 1. Stitch through last bead in Row 3. Continue.

Method 2: Simple Cheat

Stitch through the last two beads from your starting row. Pick up one bead and stitch back through the second bead from the starting row and the last bead you added.

Method 3: Around the End

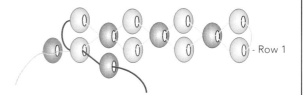

- Row 1

Perhaps the simplest method, it's often easiest to finish the odd end by continuing to stitch around the end, beginning your new row on the opposite side of your starting line.

Increases and Decreases

Peyote Stitch Increases

Peyote stitch increases widen your bead work and can be used to fill in odd gaps in freeform peyote. They are also essential to ruffles. Increases are worked over the course of two rows.

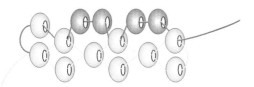

In the first row, add two beads where you would normally add one (the increase pairs are shaded darker blue in the sample above).

add an extra bead between each pair

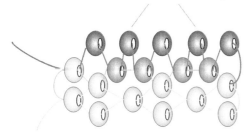

In the second row, add a single bead in between each bead pair. Be careful not to split your previous stitches and pull each bead tight.

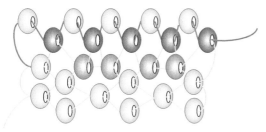

Continue working peyote stitch as normal, adding one bead in between each bead from the previous row.

Peyote Stitch Decreases

Peyote stitch decreases narrow your bead work and can also be used to fill in odd gaps in freeform peyote. Decreases are also worked over the course of two rows.

Stitch through 2 beads

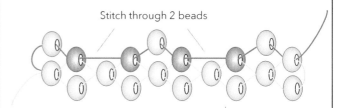

In the first row, stitch through two beads without adding a new bead. Then continue normally unless you want more decreases. (The sample above has the start of two decreases, both shaded darker blue).

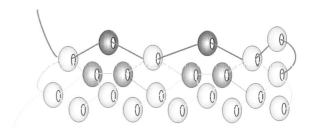

In the next row, add a single bead above each decrease pair. Adjust the tension to help ease the transition to prevent your beading from buckling.

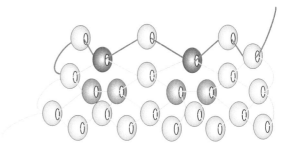

Continue working peyote stitch as normal, adding one bead in between each bead from the previous row.

Tubular Peyote: Peyote Stitch in the Round

Circular peyote is particularly useful for creating beaded rings, cords, tubes and other cylindrical objects.

Step 1 - String a ring of beads, circling through the loop at least twice. Coming up out of the loop, pick up a bead and begin peyote stitch - skipping one bead in the loop and stitching through the next. Continue around the loop.

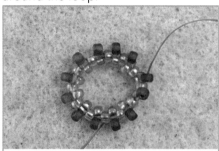

The first couple of circles will want to splay out. Expect this and keep a tight tension.

As you continue to stitch, the beads will begin to pull in to form a hollow tube.

It can also help to use a dowel or other cylindrical object to help form the shape.

Even Count Circular Peyote

starting circle 12 beads

peyote stitch around the ring

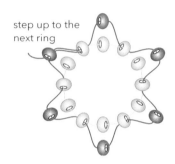

step up to the next ring

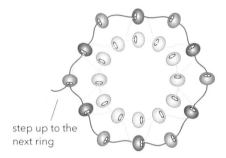

step up to the next ring

Step 2 - Even Count: If you started with an even number of beads, finish each circle by stitching through the first bead from your original circle, then your first bead from the ring you just completed.

At the end of each ring, you will stitch through two beads - the last bead of the previous ring and the first bead of the ring you just completed.

Odd Count Circular Peyote

starting circle 9 beads

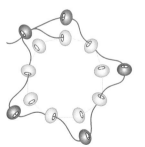

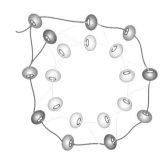

Step 2 - Odd Count: If you strung an odd number of beads, finish the circle by stitching through the first bead of the ring you just completed. It looks a bit lopsided at first, but you won't have to watch for the step up.

Notes on Beading Thread

The way I see it, my beading thread should do double or triple duty. At a minimum, the thread needs to be strong, resistant to splits and tangles, and extremely flexible; but as thin as possible so that I can fit multiple stitches through each bead. I also like it to feel soft and pliable like sewing thread.

Beading Thread as a Design Element

Ideally, the thread should also help further my design. My goal isn't simply to make the thread 'invisible', but to make sure that it actively furthers my color message.

This is why I prefer to use the colored beading threads currently on the market. I actively use their colors to help shade my beads and carry my color message.

Take a look at the two peyote stitch thread samplers below. In each row I used a particular color of transparent or semi-transparent beads. The columns were stitched using different colors of thread. My goal was to see how the different thread colors affected the apparent colors of my beads. The yellow and white rows at the bottom are inside-color beads, not completely transparent.

My Thread Suggestions

One-G™ - a mono-filament nylon thread, One-G seems slightly stronger and less prone to splitting stitches than Superlon. This is my new favorite beading thread; however, it does not come in as many colors as Superlon.

Superlon AA™ - another mono-filament nylon thread, I find Superlon easier to work with than Nymo. I recommend always using the finer size (AA) of Superlon for freeform peyote.

Silamide™ - a twisted, waxed nylon thread, Silamide is extremely strong and fairly resistant to split stitches. You can find it in larger spools or cardboard cards. I don't use this thread very often any more, but would still recommend it if it were what your local bead store carried.

Fireline™ - I seldom use Fireline in my freeform as I find even the 4lb too thick for the number of thread passes I tend to make through my beading. It is useful if you are working primarily with crystals or bugle beads that might have sharp edges which could cut other threads.

Changing Threads

Wherever possible, I prefer to weave my thread tails into my work rather than using a knot when changing threads. Knots aren't nearly as secure as you might expect. If you've ever had a knot come undone as you tried to stitch through the beads around it, you know what I mean. Worse, knots can create blockages, making it very difficult to stitch through those beads later.

Instead, I prefer to weave my thread tails into my work. To make sure your thread tail is secure, change stitching directions at least two to three times before clipping your thread. The diagrams at right show this in a three-step process.

The thread may show a little where you change directions. For this reason I suggest working from the back of your piece when changing threads wherever possible. This helps to minimize the visibility of your beading thread on the front of your piece.

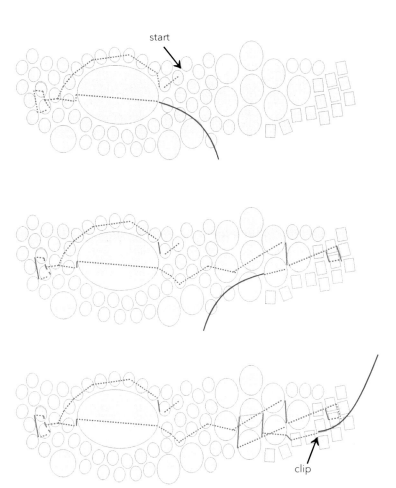

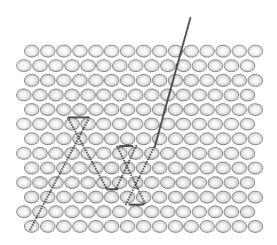

Weaving a thread tail into regular peyote stitch

The diagram above shows four direction changes. Three of the changes are crossovers, where I stitched back through the same bead.

Photos on opposite page: above right: spools of Superlon beading thread; below right: One-G spools in two sizes; below left: stitch samples showing the effect of thread colors on transparent beads.

Weaving a thread tail into freeform peyote stitch

Weaving your tails into freeform peyote can be a little more complicated because you need to find good places to change directions. The direction changes and crossovers are just as important here.

Larger beads make great pass-throughs because of their larger thread holes, however they are not as secure a place for direction changes for the same reason. I like to make sure that at least a couple of my direction changes happen in my size 11° beads.

Basic Tools

There are relatively few tools that I consider truly essential. Below is a quick list of my personal favorites and why.

Needles - I prefer to work with Sharps rather than standard beading needles. I find it easier to wedge the shorter needles into the often tight and awkward angles of freeform peyote without worrying about breakage. Think of the difference in turning radius for a little sports car compared to a school bus. I work with size 11s in general and size 12s when the 11s are too thick.

Curved Beading Needles are sometimes the only way to go when you're working on a sculptural form.

Scissors - small, sharp embroidery scissors that narrow down to as sharp a point as possible are the best! I sometimes use a thread burner, but the embroidery scissors are more portable.

Bead Mat - because I often bead on the go, I prefer to use a thin Vellux™ beading mat. I've collected a variety of sizes, but each is about 3/8" thick and folds up nicely. I love the way my beads sit on the surface, waiting to be picked up, but less likely to roll around and escape.

Bead Scoop - at the studio I use a little metal tray in the shape of a triangle. For travel, the best bead scoop I've found is a gelato spoon with a squared scoop. Really!

Thread Cutter - for plane travel, I leave my embroidery scissors safely at home and take a round thread cutter instead. So far, I've never had a problem with security and often bead while in flight. (It's a great conversation starter.)

Pliers - I use a miniature pair of pliers to help pull my needle through tight bead holes. A word of caution - you have to use these with care because if the bead holes are too tight then you can break your bead as you pull the needle through with the pliers. Use the pliers to save your hands from a little extra grunt work rather than to attempt the impossible.

Beeswax - depending upon the beading thread you choose to use, beeswax is useful to help strengthen the thread and keep it from shredding. I especially like to use it when I'm working with Superlon, but have been known to wax One-G as well depending upon what else I'm working with.

Freeform Peyote Techniques

Freeform Peyote is Abstract, not Random, Organic, rather than strictly geometric. Think of the way tree roots grow into the soil, or cream swirls into hot coffee; one sinuous shape melding into the next. Those are some of my personal guideposts in freeform design.

Seed beads are the basis for most, if not all, freeform peyote creations, just as with other forms of bead weaving. Size 11°s (or sometimes 8°s), generally form the bulwark of the designs while larger seed beads, shaped seed beads, accent beads and focals add contrast and spark.

While we work with the basic idea of peyote stitch to hold our bead weaving together, I suggest you let go of many of the hard and fast rules of standard bead weaving. Instead, we will focus on what each piece itself needs to grow from a skinny little twig of a starting line of beads to blossom into an original freeform design.

Working along the Length

This method is most commonly used for bracelets, but can be used with any freeform peyote.

With this method, start by stringing beads equal to the full length of your piece. If you plan to use a button & loop closure, string the button loop as part of the starting length.

I typically change colors or bead type every one to two inches. Make sure to vary the lengths of each bead type for a more organic composition. This allows you to establish your main color blocks immediately.

Work proceeds along the length, transitioning back and forth from one bead type and color to the next as you work.

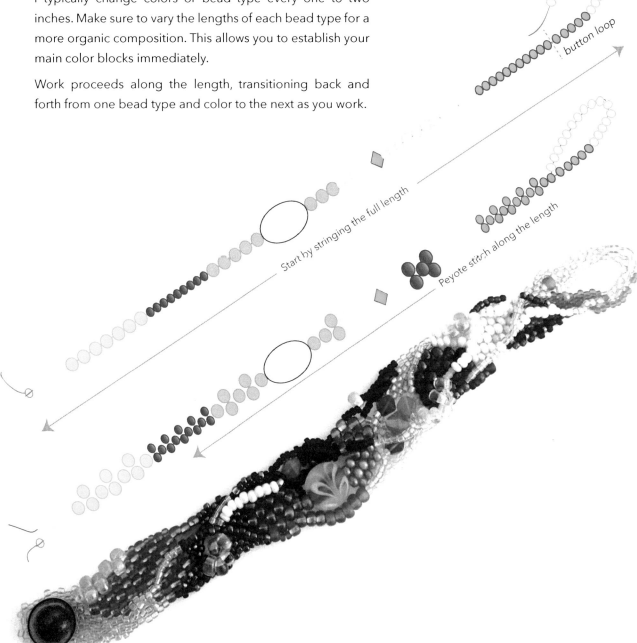

button loop

Start by stringing the full length

Peyote stitch along the length

Working along the Width

While working along the width is very common in regular peyote stitch patterns, it's considerably more unusual in freeform peyote.

With this method, start by stringing beads equal to roughly the intended final width of your piece. Your starting length will be relatively short.

Working along the width, you can start from one end and work towards the other, or from the middle and work out towards either end.

Internal bridges will be shorter as they will cross the width of your piece instead of the length. In her bracelet below, Ibolya Barkóczi uses a series of short bridges to create an open, lattice effect in several sections.

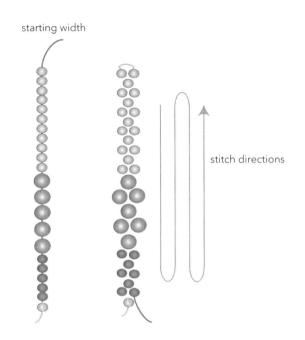

starting width

stitch directions

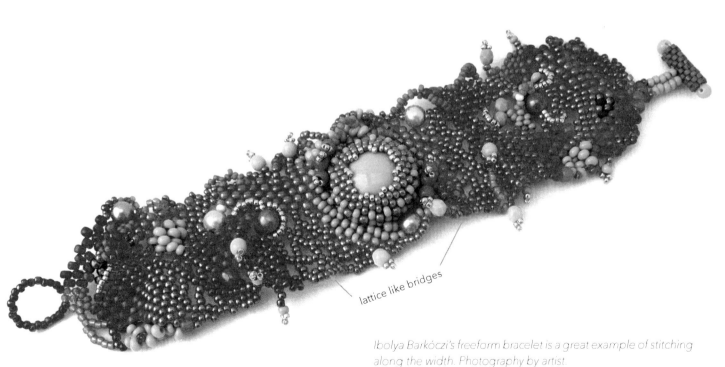

lattice like bridges

Ibolya Barkóczi's freeform bracelet is a great example of stitching along the width. Photography by artist.

Building Bridges

Creating New Paths

Once you've established your basic line of beading, you may choose to add alternate bead paths. These alternate lines of beading can introduce windows and paths into your beading, act as course corrections, help frame larger focals and generally add visual and textural interest.

To create a bridge, exit from your main line of beading, pick up sufficient beads to span the desired gap and stitch back into your bead weaving. In subsequent rows you may choose to leave those beads as a solitary line or work peyote stitch off of their edge.

working along the length first four rows.

little bridges circle accent beads

alternate bead path bridges. Left open to create showcase windows for 12mm beads.

later bridge to frame the 12mm Czech beads

smaller bridges frame 4mm fire-polished beads

Minimizing Lumps & Bumps

When transitioning between different bead types and sizes, small lumps and bumps are almost inevitable. However, you can minimize the effects by modifying your peyote stitch to better accommodate the differing sizes. Forget about adding a single bead with each stitch. Instead, add the beads necessary to fit the space you need to fill.

When transitioning from larger beads to smaller, you may need to use more than one bead to fill the available space. Czech seed beads are particularly useful here; their lack of uniformity in width allows you to pick just the right size or sizes to fill each space.

When transitioning from smaller beads to larger, you may need to skip a stitch point or more to fit the larger bead in smoothly. I often find it helpful to add the larger beads in groups of twos or threes to better bridge the space.

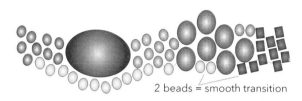

When transitioning to smaller beads, you may need to use more than one bead to fill the space smoothly.

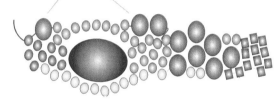

When transitioning to larger beads, you may need to skip a stitch or two in your bead weaving to make a smooth transition.

A curving bump of lime-green seed beads becomes a half bezel for a 12mm accent bead.

Design Tip: Sometimes, no matter how careful you are, a bulge will start to appear. This is especially true when you're first experimenting with freeform peyote.

You could back out several rows of stitching and try again, or you can find a way to incorporate that bulge into your design.

One of my favorite ways to make such occurrences work for me is to use them to wrap around a larger accent bead. Use a short bridge to draw your previous beading up around one side of your accent bead and you have an instant half bezel!

Working around Curves

When working around curves you must learn to adjust your beading to fit. Just like on a racetrack, there is more distance to cover along the outer edge of the curve than the inner.

If you try to fill either space using the exact same size and number of beads that you used for your first line, then you will build a curving wall, stacking beads vertically rather than to the side. This can be useful if you're trying to create a bezel or a beaded rope and is the basis behind tubular peyote stitch.

To create a flat curve, you must either change the size or number of beads you use to fit. Czech beads, with their varying widths, can be very useful here.

This process photo, taken during the construction of my Winter Blues cuff, contains several flat curves, including three depicted with arrows. Note how I altered my bead counts to accommodate the varying degrees of curve.

Working along Inner and Outer Curves

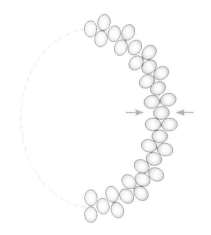

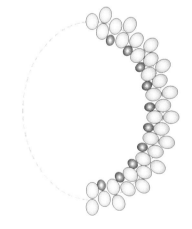

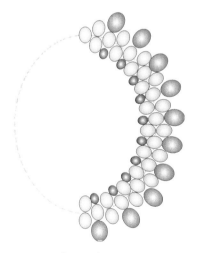

Take a look at the difference in size of the spaces between the beads along the inner and outer edges.

The spaces along the inner edge are considerably smaller and require smaller beads or perhaps even decreases to fit the curve smoothly.

The spaces along the outer curve are much larger. Note that the sharper the curve (top/bottom), the larger the gaps between beads.

Building a Flat Spiral

This earring sample gives a quick look at shaping both inner and outer curves.

175% actual size

The goal here was to create sinuous-but-flat, spiraling curves.

For the outer curves, I used a combination of peyote stitch increases and larger beads, first adding size 8°s, then size 6°s.

Along the inner curves, I used decreases where necessary to help with shaping. I did not step down to smaller beads, although I could have chosen to do so.

Standard peyote stitch. The green 6° helps identify the center point.

I added increases in an alternating path along the outer edges. The light brown arrows show where I stitched through my beading to change sides.

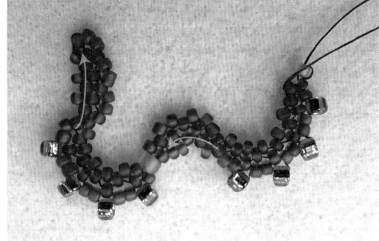

Working along the bottom edge, I added larger, 8° seed beads in the gaps along the outer curves and stitched through the inner curves to help shape them.

21

Using the Elements of Design as Guideposts

Value

Contrast

Texture

Line

Color

At different points in my life, I managed some fluency in both Spanish and Russian as well as maintaining a reasonable command of my native English. Learning new languages always drives home two points for me:

1) Use it or loose it - if you stop practicing a language, it becomes more and more difficult to use it with any fluency.

2) Our language frames and shapes our thoughts, and different languages make it easier to think about different things.

The vocabulary of design makes it easier to analyze and interpret what you see, and to transform inspiration into original designs through a series of conscious decisions. Over the next few pages, I will share a quick overview of my working vocabulary pertaining to the abstract art form that is freeform peyote.

Teasing apart the various elements of design so that we can look at each separately can be tricky because they're all so closely intertwined. Each is affected by the others. This is particularly the case with value and contrast. That said, I'm going to do my best to tease them apart and look at each separately.

Speaking of value and contrast, I've removed the color information from the lower left side of Sarah Meadows' *Fiesta* necklace to make it easier to see the Value Contrast separately from the color. Note how even in her red-on-red rosette, Sarah uses value for added interest.

Fiesta, by Sarah Meadows.
Photography by W. John MacMullen.

Value

What is Value? The best definition I've come up with is that value describes the quality(ies) of lightness or darkness in a particular object or composition. When people in the design industry talk about value, they use terms like "high" and "low" instead of light and dark. I'll use both sets of terminology here.

High Values are very light values shading to the white end of the value scale. **Low Values** refers to very dark values shading all the way to black.

Medium Values refer to (you guessed it) values somewhere in the middle of the scale between light and dark.

Why is Value important?

1) Value carries an emotional impact. Adjectives such as 'light and airy' or 'dark and mysterious' convey these concepts.

2) Value helps direct your eye through a composition. Our eyes are drawn to lighter, brighter objects first.

3) Value contrast helps us differentiate between the various elements in a composition.

To discuss the relationship of how the differing values in a composition work together, we use the term **Contrast**.

High Value Contrast pieces contain a wide range of values from light to dark. The greater the value differences, the greater the contrast. A black and white composition, like a chessboard, has strong value contrast.

In **Low Value Contrast compositions** all of the values cluster in one section of the value scale - high, medium or low. Pastels are a great example of a high value composition with low value-contrast.

With its pastel palette, Marlene Oman Emmons' 'Carrie' bracelet is a high value, low value contrast composition. Photography by Christie Captain Photography.

'Spanish Dancer' has a range of medium values, with medium value contrast.

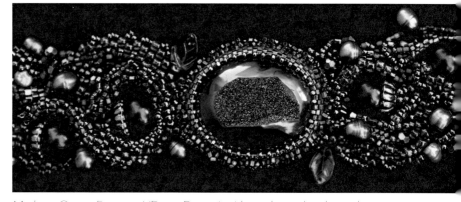

Marlene Oman Emmons' 'Druzy Dreaming' has a low value, low value contrast composition. Photography by Christie Captain Photography.

Physical Texture

The dictionary defines texture as "the visual and especially tactile quality of a surface" and as "the characteristic structure of the interwoven or intertwined threads, strands or the like that make up a tactile fabric". We are interested in the tactile fabric that created from freeform bead weaving, the texture of which is determined in part by the qualities of the individual beads that make up the whole. When we use beads that are smooth, coarse, lumpy, ridges, rounded, squared, etc., all of these different surface textures contribute to the whole.

Changing the Scale

The use of different sizes and shapes of beads (and bead-like objects) is one of the hallmarks of freeform peyote. By changing the scale, we alter the physical texture of our work. The smooth, polished plains of traditional peyote give way to the more textured terrain of freeform.

Contrast vs. Cohesiveness

In order to create a pleasing composition, you need to have elements that work as a unifying force and those which provide contrast. Too much contrast and the design disappears into chaos. Too strong a unifying force and the composition looses visual interest.

Smooth Rough Sharp
Flat Bumpy Lumpy
Coarse Fine Polished
Big Small Tiny
Square Round Irregular
Glass Stone Acrylic

Lampworked beads by Juli Cannon of Jules Beads

Seed Beads - the basic building blocks

The base 'fabric' of most freeform peyote designs is composed of size 11° (or sometimes size 8°) seed beads. Within each size designation, there's a surprising range of actual sizes and physical textures that we can take advantage of in our freeform compositions.

Precision-made **Delicas**™, by Miyuki of Japan, create a smooth, perfectly even surface.

The size variations for which **Czech seed beads** are known creates an organic, textural surface.

In between are the **Japanese seed beads**, which tend to be slightly larger physically than either of the other two varieties. They also tend to have the largest thread holes, making them ideal for areas of your piece that may require intensive stitching.

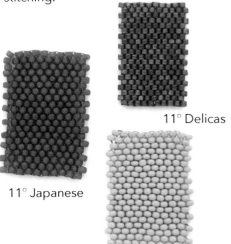

11° Japanese

Each stitch sample = 20 rows

11° Delicas

11° Czech

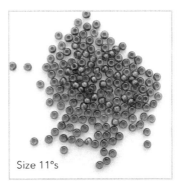

Size 11°s

Size 8°s

Size 6°s

Crow beads

Rizos

1.5mm cubes

Size 8° hexs

SuperDuos

Magatamas

Tilas

3° bugles

3.4mm drops

Visual Texture

Visual Texture allows us to talk about how our eyes react to the surface finishes of the beads and findings we use. While not physically discernible, our eyes react very differently to a transparent object than to an opaque object of the same color and value.

Look at the surface finishes of Lisa's *Spring!* bracelet, her very first piece of freeform. From the high-gloss opacity of her agate focal, to the transparent crystals tucked into grottoes of matte and metallic seed beads, she blends visual textures into a whole. Glossy, soft-pink-lined, minty green seed beads add another layer of subtle visual texture.

Spring! bracelet by Lisa Jones. Take a look at the variety of surface textures and the finishes of the beads Lisa chose for her spring-themed bracelet. Photography by artist.

Matte   Metallic

Transparent

Opaque Iris

Opalescent

Shiny   Rainbow

Inside Color

Line

Just like in everyday life, lines tell us where to go, when to stop, where to pause. A continuous line will quickly draw the viewer's eyes through a composition like a fast moving stream; while a line that disappears and reappears through the composition creates pools where the eye can rest before traveling on.

In your beading, you can 'draw' lines using value, color, size or even texture. It's a good idea to decide on one primary method of 'drawing'. In my work, I most commonly use color, supported by value and scale, to create the sense of flow.

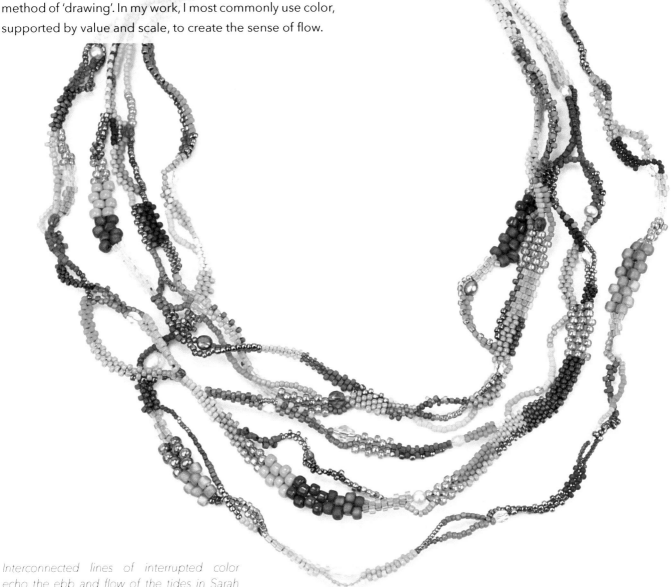

Interconnected lines of interrupted color echo the ebb and flow of the tides in Sarah Meadows' simple, yet striking necklace, 'Ocean'. Photography by W. John MacMullen.

Working with the Color Wheel

We've all seen Color Wheels before. Most have a lovely rainbow of colors like the one at left including:

Primary colors: red, yellow, and blue.

Secondary colors: orange, green and purple/violet.

Tertiary colors: (sandwiched between the primary and secondary colors): red-orange, yellow-orange, yellow-green, blue-green, blue-violet, and red-violet.

We all know the drill.

The key is understanding how to use the Color Wheel to develop our own color combinations and palettes.

The Color Wheel is simply a tool to help us better understand the relationships between the various colors found on the wheel. Because all the colors on a particular wheel are defined by their relationships, you could say that they are one great big color family, bound by a number of familial traits.

The traits which link the colors on the wheel include Value, Intensity, Undertones, and Color Temperature. By experimenting with these traits uniformly around the color wheel we can study and develop alternate Color Wheel Families. The key is to apply the changes uniformly to all the colors around the wheel while obeying a few simple rules. That way all of the color relationships remain the same.

For instance, yellow is always the lightest color and violet the darkest in terms of value on any given color wheel. So if you decide to create a color wheel of pastels, you'd need to keep this in mind. If your violet somehow ended up lighter than the yellow, it simply wouldn't look right for that color wheel.

Tips for Building Your Own Color Wheel:

Value: As noted above, purple is always darkest (has the lowest value); while yellow is always lightest. Also, the red and green should have approximately the same relative values.

Color Temperature: Orange is always the hottest color in any particular color wheel. Blue is always the coolest. Again, if you create a color wheel that breaks this rule, it simply won't look right.

Intensity: All of the colors in the wheel should have approximately the same relative intensity.

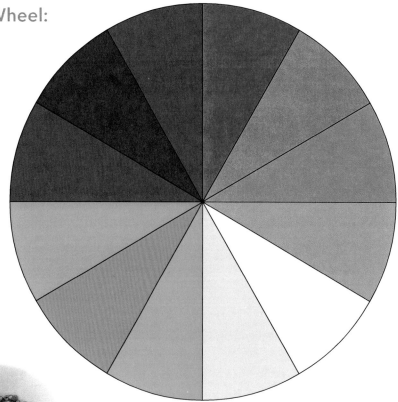

In the traditional color wheel pictured above and the bead sampler wheel on the facing page at far left, all of the colors are fully intense versions of their base colors.

The bead color wheel to the near left is based more on earth tones. All of the colors are less intense, with warm undertones.

Color Temperature

Hot, Hot, Hot or Not, Not, Not

Sunny yellows, red hot, cool blue - every color has an associated Color Temperature.

Working around the color wheel, those in the red to yellow range are warm colors. While the blues, greens and purples are generally regarded as cool colors. Seems simple enough, right?

It gets a little more complicated than that, unfortunately; because the Color Temperature of a particular color is also affected by the colors around it.

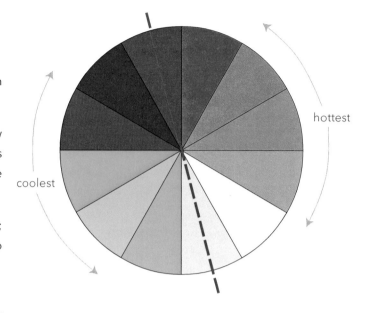

hottest

coolest

Color Temperature Fluctuates on the Cusps

Red-violet and yellow-green - colors on the cusps between the warm and cool colors - sometimes seem warm and sometimes cool. Because they're stuck halfway between the warm and cool colors, they don't really know which side of the family they belong. They shift their apparent color temperature dramatically based upon who they're paired up with.

Just to be contrary, they tend to take the opposite Color Temperature from the majority in any combination. Kind of like reverse camouflage.

So, if they're paired with warm colors - lots of reds, oranges and yellows, they'll seem cool. Snuggled in with cool blues, greens and violets, they suddenly turn warm.

Check out the lime green and magenta beads in the photographs at left - they're the same in both photographs. But their apparent Color Temperature is not.

Understanding Undertones & Intensity

Undertones: The Hidden Message

Then there are Undertones. Here's where we get into cool and warm Hues of the same color.

Varying the undertones can create Temperature differences even within the same color family, such as the blues bead sampler to the right. Blues with strong red Undertones tend to appear warmer, while those with green Undertones will seem much cooler in comparison.

This is one way to increase interest in monochromatic compositions. Undertones can also explain why different hues of the same color simply don't seem to go together.

Intensity

Intensity allows us to look at the relative clarity of a particular hue in reference to its base primary color. Primary colors are fully intense examples of their basic hues (primary red, blue and yellow). In the print industry, Intensity is referred to as Saturation.

When we use adjectives such as bright, rich, dull or muted to describe a hue, what we are usually trying to convey is its relative Intensity (or lack thereof).

Working with paint, you can alter the Intensity of a hue without changing its Value in one of two ways:

1) Add in just a smidgen of its complimentary color. So, if you're working with red, then add just a touch of green.

2) Mix in a neutral grey of the same relative value. As the grey is the same value as your color, it will reduce the intensity without changing the value.

The apparent value of a hue can be affected by its Intensity. For instance, hues with a low intensity will often appear darker than a similar, more intense hue.

Monochromatic Creations

All in the Family

I like to think of the varying shades and tones of a single color as siblings within a particular color family, each inheriting a series of traits from its parent hue.

Designing with a single color family works as a strong unifying element.

Contrast must come from somewhere else. Both examples on this page make liberal use of Value for this purpose; including light, dark and mid-tones in their designs.

Variations in Texture and Scale can also provide the necessary contrast, especially when working with a narrow range of Values.

Left: In the Pink necklace by Mary Kearney. Photography by artist.

Below: Ocean Waves bracelet by author.

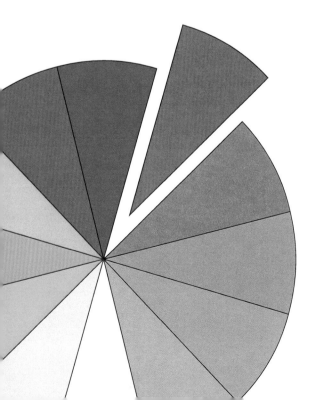

Analogous Colors

Near Neighbors

Analogous Colors are next door neighbors on the color wheel. They go together quite naturally due to their close proximity.

In fact, sometimes it can be hard to decide where one color leaves off and the next begins. That's where the 12-step color wheel comes in handy.

Both of the samples on this page span a good section of the color wheel. Marsha Melone's *Seafoam* necklace shades from soft pink, through orangey, buttery yellows to a soft minty green, all in delicate, pastel hues. Meanwhile my *Spanish Dancer* bracelet employs bold hues from yellowy orange through the reds to deep violet.

Above Right: Seafoam necklace by Marsha Melone. Photography by artist.

Below: Spanish Dancer bracelet by author.

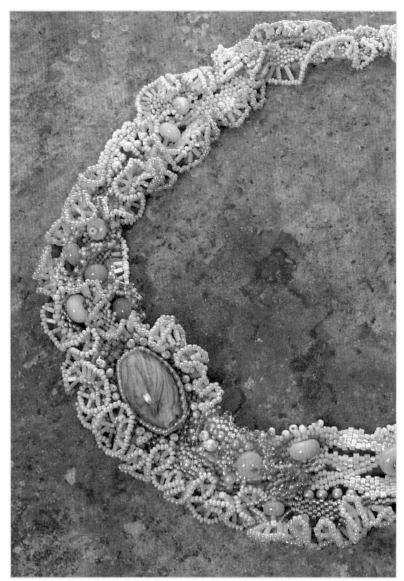

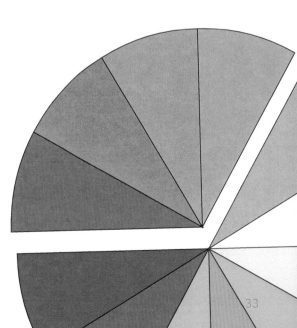

Complimentary Creatior

Opposites Attract

Like Summer and Winter, complimentary color designs draw both warm and cool temperatures into play. You're pulling not only from opposite sides of the color wheel, but also from opposing color temperatures.

Take the Blue/Orange compliments: here you're combining orange, the hottest color on the color wheel, with blue the coolest. This makes for a particularly dynamic color scheme, but also poses its own set of problems as the two vie for dominance. In her freeform necklace at right, Jennifer Porter allows the reds to dominate, using green as accents and secondary focal points.

Right: detail, Colors in Late Winter necklace by Jennifer Porter.

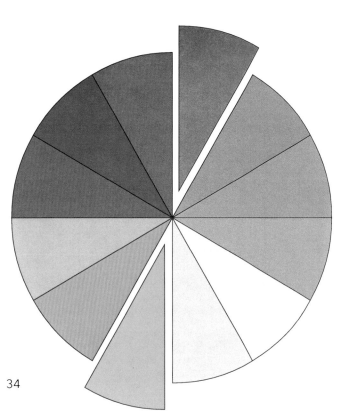

Value/Temperature Pairings:

Orange and Blue: some value contrast, strong color temperature differences.

Purple and Yellow/Gold: strong value contrast, some color temperature differences.

Red and Green: smallest value contrast of the complimentary combinations, some color temperature contrast.

Triadic Creations

Three's Company

Spaced evenly around the color wheel, triadic combinations draw from three separate color families.

Triadic combinations are beautifully balanced. The primary colors - red, blue and yellow - form one of the most widely known triads. The secondary colors - green, violet and orange - form another.

In her *Trilogy in Peyote* collar, Ellen Lambright uses a slightly modified triad, substituting a soft silvery gold for yellow. The palette for my *Peacock Spring* bracelet is a triad of tertiary colors.

Above Right: detail, Trilogy in Peyote collar by Ellen Lambright.

Below: Peacock Spring bracelet by author.

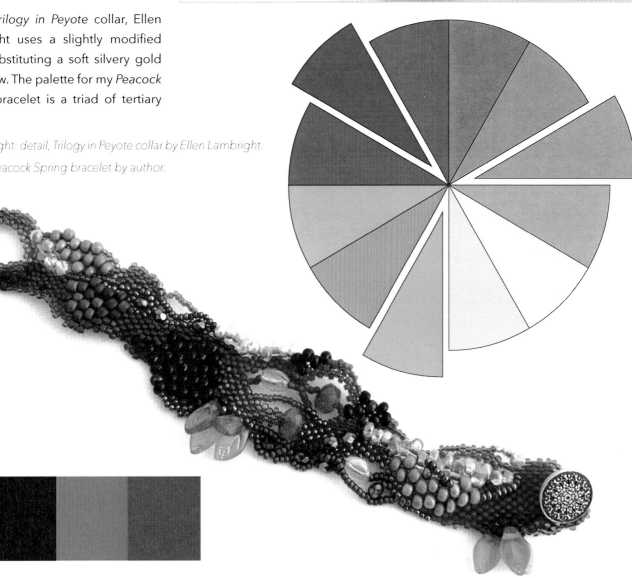

Expanding on a Theme

Once you have invested the time and energy collecting beads for a color scheme you love, why not have fun with it and make several pieces before moving on to to another? You could make a 'traditional' jewelry set - coordinating earrings, bracelet, necklace, etc. Or you can work in a series creating the same style of piece, but exploring different ways of combining your palette.

I find that this can help me feel less overwhelmed when trying to decide where to get started. Because I know that I'll have an opportunity to try out additional ideas in the 'next' piece I make, it relieves the anxiety that I have to choose 'the right' place to start. There really is no 'right' way, but this means that rather than sorting through too many ideas for a single piece, I translate the inspiration into fodder for multiple pieces.

CHAPTER TWO

Little Beauties

Freeform Earrings

Simple Earrings

The fastest freeform peyote projects I know of, freeform earrings are a great way to experiment with a variety of colors, techniques and bead combinations.

Rather than trying to make a matching pair, freeform earrings simply need to coordinate. The simplest way to coordinate designs is to use the same bead types and sizes in both earrings, but change their placement and your stitching paths. Try out different ideas for each earring, working with your theme. This will give you a nice balance between contrast and cohesiveness.

I don't like to have to change thread while making earrings, so I start out with a longer than normal length; forty eight to sixty inches (48-60"). After you've made a couple of earrings, you can adjust your starting length based upon your general usage.

Earring One

I started by stringing a stop bead then a length of seed beads with two larger accents - a lampworked bead by artist JJ Jacobs and a stone disc. The total length is approximately one and a half inches (1 1/2"), so relatively short.

Working peyote stitch back along the length to my starting point; I stitched through both of the larger, accent beads. I will stitch around them both in later rows, right now it's more important to make sure they are secure.

Over the next two rows, I added bridges to either side of the stone disc. I peyote stitched down to the disc, then bridged to the left. Peyote stitching around the bottom, I then strung a new bridge heading up along the right.

I worked peyote stitch along the edge of the arching, blue bridge.

About this point, the earring started to remind me of a leaf, so I decided to run with that idea.

I added some open lines of stitching along the right edge using 15°s to balance things out.

I then added 4mm crystal rondelles in each of the gaps and a crystal picot to finish off the bottom.

Last, I added a silver-plated earring hook, stitching down into the earring to secure my thread.

A closeup of finished earring on a white background.

Earring Two

I started the second earring very similarly to the first, but note the color differences. I also added the turn bead/ picot to the bottom immediately this time around.

After working bridges to either side of the stone bead, I again began working peyote stitch along the left edge.

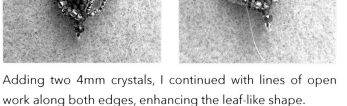

Adding two 4mm crystals, I continued with lines of open work along both edges, enhancing the leaf-like shape.

Adding the earring hook to the finished piece.

Finished earring with JJ Jacob's lampworked bead.

Flame Leaves

This is a semi-freeform project where there is a basic pattern that could be repeated exactly, or you can take the idea of the pattern and play with it to create a series of similar, but unique flame leaves. All bead counts are flexible! Hence semi-freeform. I won't provide specific bead counts, but will give suggestions.

Depending upon the colors used, these little beauties remind me of flames, leaves, feathers or even flower petals. They can also take on a distinct heart-shape if you continue building the shape (second from right in bottom row).

The flame leaves can make cute earrings by themselves, or you can incorporate them into larger projects.

Constructing the Leaves

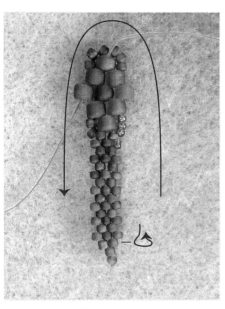

Starting Rows. String a stop bead. Pick up five to seven (5-7) 6°s and about seventeen 11° seed beads.

Reverse directions, stitching back through the second to last bead. Work peyote stitch back up along the length, matching bead types.

Rows 4 & 5. Working in a circular fashion, stitch up along one side and then down the other.

Do not stitch all the way to the point. For rows four and five, change directions at the last pair of beads. Above, create a diamond shape with the 6°s.

Rows 6 & 7. Working two rows along the left-hand side, I changed direction four beads from the bottom.

The inset shows the thread path I used to change directions.

Start outlining the 6°s with the smaller size 11°s.

Rows 8 & 9. Work the next two rows along the right-hand side. Note the short bridge I used to add a 4mm crystal accent toward the top.

Rows 10 & 11. Stitching over the top to add two more rows to the left-hand side, along with another crystal accent bead.

Continuing to switch back and forth over the top of the leaf. I added a short bridge outlining the crystal on the right.

Beads List

~2g each, 2-3 colors size 11°s

~1-2g 6°s or other similarly sized beads

Optional: 8°s, 4mm crystals or fire-polished beads, triangle beads, etc.

My green leaf has two different size 11° beads - emerald frosted AB and transparent teal.

Nearly done - how many more rows to add depends upon how wide we wish the final leaf shape to be.

I like to clean up the outer edges, filling any major gaps, before calling it complete.

Remember that these design notes are just a jumping off point for further explorations! Have fun experimenting with bead counts and your favorite bead types.

Winter Flame Earrings

I designed these earrings during a week-long snowstorm several years ago. Shading from a deep ultramarine blue to a bright, sunny yellow, the colors and shape evoke the cheery warmth of a candle flame.

Notes on Color Blending

String a stop bead, then pick up five to seven (5-7) dark blue size 6° beads. Pick up two to three (2-3) beads of each of the colors you plan to use in your flame leaf, shading through the colors in a progression. I used cobalt blue; inside-color deep purple; transparent red; inside-color hot magenta; transparent orange; matte transparent orange; and transparent yellow.

With each row, move the colors up towards the larger beads, creating v-shaped bands of color. Some colors (like the magenta) may only sweep to one side or the other. You're mimicking flames here, so it shouldn't be too regular.

Allow the transparent yellow to creep up around the outer edges of your flame leaf. Not as a solid outline, but in stops and starts.

Lotus Blossom Hair Ornament

I decided it would be fun to work my flame leaves into a larger project. This festive, lotus-inspired hair ornament was the result.

Playing with Design Options

At first all I knew was that I wanted to create a larger design. I'd stitched a number of leaf shapes, but didn't know what I wanted to do with them or how many I needed. Rather than continuing to stitch randomly, I needed some direction.

So I decided to step back and play with design options using paper cut-outs - a quick alternative to sketching.

I used colored pages torn from magazines, store-bought colored papers and some papers I'd hand-painted with dye. All that really mattered were the colors!

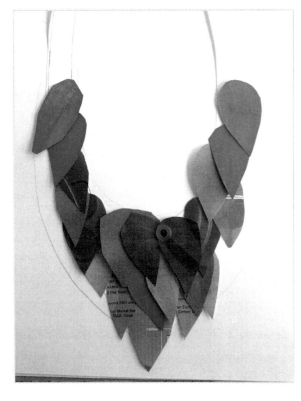

Playing with the collage, I quickly decided I didn't want to make a collar (collage at left) - it seemed a bit too heavy.

Arranging the leaves in a layered half circle, they transformed into the petals of a lotus blossom. I decided to make a hair ornament.

Assembling the Hair Ornament

After stitching all the petals, I gathered the rest of the supplies; including buckram, interfacing, hand-dyed cotton fabric and Ultrasuede.

Sandwiching the buckram between two layers of interfacing, I hand-basted the dyed cotton over the sandwich to create my foundation.

With my paper collage as a guide, I stitched the petals in place one at a time using the remaining construction thread from each petal.

In the end, I stopped with the red petals.

47

Simple Ring with Crystal Focal

Beads List

~2g each, 4-6 colors size 11°s

~1-2g each, 8°s or 10° triangles or other similarly sized beads

1 12mm crystal rondelle (or similarly sized bead)

Optional: 4mm crystals or fire-polished beads as accents

Remember that these are simply suggestions. This is a great place to experiment with all of the new shaped beads on the market. Most of all - have fun!

Building a Ring

Measure out thirty six to forty eight inches (36-48") of beading thread.

String a stop bead. String enough beads to fit *loosely* around the base of your finger or a sizing rod if you prefer. Place your crystal or focal bead about halfway along the length. Circle through the first bead to create a loop. Stitch through the entire circle a second time for stability.

Tip: The initial ring of beads should be a loose fit, It will get tighter as you stitch. How much tighter depends upon the techniques you decide to use.

The ring should fit loosely at this point.

Facing page: Emerald City Ring by Lisa Jones. Photography by artist.
Lisa surrounded her crystal focal with several lines of stacked beads.

Work peyote stitch around the circle. Stitch through the bead on either side of the crystal and the crystal itself.

Keep your tension tight, but don't worry if your beading flares out a little. That will straighten itself out as you continue to stitch.

Pick up enough beads to create a bridge around one side of the crystal.

Do not make the bridge too tight as it will draw in even further if you decide to work peyote stitch along the bridge.

Continue working peyote stitch in the round.

In the photo above, I have just finished my first row of peyote stitch along the right-side bridge, creating a faux bezel for my crystal focal. There is an odd-shaped gap where the bridge meets the band - a perfect spot to tuck an accent bad.

Continuing to work peyote stitch off of either side.

Note: The back of your ring should be no more than five to six rows wide - enough to provide stability, but still narrow enough to be comfortable to wear.

Trying on the ring while in process. This often makes it easier to see what is still necessary.

The upper left edge has a concave curve to it that I don't like. Definitely want to fill that in.

Using some of the silver-lined size 8°s to fill in the hollow along the upper left.

Also notice the diagonal line of beading running across the surface.

Baby Spikes Rings

The blue ring boasts five short spike beads (each 4.5 x 8mm) arranged in two rows.

You can also make the ring with seven spikes arranged in three rows like the lavender ring shown in the insert above.

Building the Ring

String a stop bead. Pick up enough beads to loosely fit your desired ring size.

I strung three size 11° seed beads between each of the three black spike beads.

Starting to work peyote stitch around the ring; I stitched straight through the front of the ring, including the seed beads between each spike for added stability.

I continued to work peyote stitch around the edge, except between the spike beads. The beads are starting to lay nicely on top of each other around the ring, now that there are several rows of peyote stitch.

Working along the top edge, I added bridges of five to six (5-6) size 11° seed beads outlining each of the spike beads along one edge.

Each bridge connects into the middle seed bead between the spikes.

I then repeated the bridges on the other edge, drawing colors in from both sides of the ring.

I needed to play with the tension a little to straighten out the bridges.

Trying on the ring. I thought it looked rather nice even at this point. Except that the bottoms of the spike beads peak out a little too much.

Time to keep stitching.

Adding two more baby spikes in a second row. I nestled each of the spikes into the hollows left between the previous spikes, using a bridge of three beads - 11° , spike bead, 11° .

The new baby spikes are to the right. Adding bridges of five to six (5-6) seed beads to outline them as well.

Almost finished. Before counting the ring as finished, I will stitch along both outer edges for greater stability and to increase the wear.

Spike Ring

Four views of a simple freeform ring with a larger glass spike bead (6.5 x 16.5mm) as the focal. Note how the beading narrows towards the back of the band, then widens to surround the spike. The shape reminds me of a traditional 'class ring', but the spike pushes it into a class all its own.

Beaded Beads
and
Personal Planets

My Personal Planets beaded beads feature freeform peyote worked over a larger center bead. I use a bamboo skewer (commonly found in kitchen supply stores) to support my bead work during construction.

Beaded Beads - Stitch Diagrams

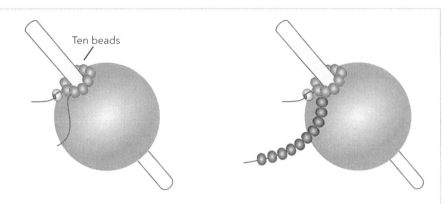

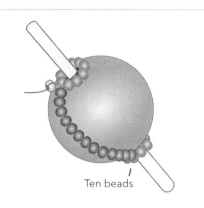

Getting Started: Slip the bamboo skewer through your base bead. For many of my designs, I use a 25-26mm round bead with a ¼" thread hole. You could use a large, blunt tapestry needle in place of the skewer.

1) String a stop bead, then ten size 11° seed beads. Circle one end of the skewer. Stitching through the circle of beads two and a half times.

2) String enough beads to reach around your base bead to the other end of the skewer like a tether. This can be any combination of bead types and sizes. Don't worry if your beading is a little loose - it will tighten as you work.

3) String ten more size 11° seed beads to circle the other end of the skewer.

Stitch through the beads around the skewer two and a half times. Do not remove the skewer! Right now it's acting as a tether, holding everything together.

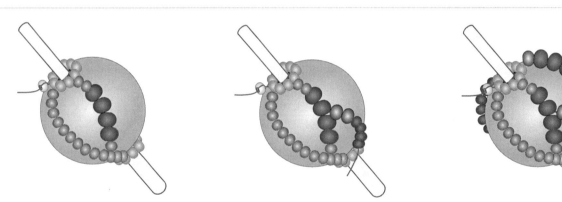

4) Create a network of bead strands connecting the two ends. At this point you're making a sort of random netting, working several lines of beads around your base bead. You will need about five to seven lines of beads around the circumference. Several of the lines should intersect.

If you're looking for a freeform beaded surface, make sure to leave space between your strands of beads, but also make sure to interconnect the strands.

> Too many lines of beads makes it harder to work peyote stitch between them. This is fine if you want a randomly netted bead, which is certainly another option, just not freeform peyote.

> Too few lines of beading, or if the lines don't intersect enough, and your beading will slip and slide as you try to stitch. The key is finding a balance.

Filling in the Blanks with Peyote Stitch

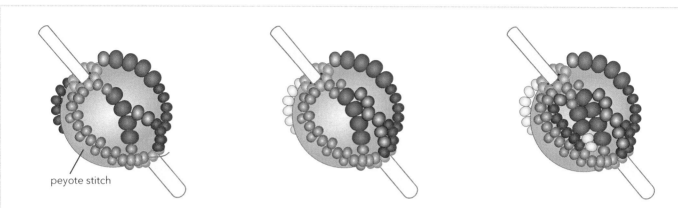

peyote stitch

Work peyote stitch off of the networked lines of beading.

Work a row of peyote stitch along one of your bead lines, matching bead types. Fill one section at a time, working back and forth like laying bricks in a wall. Or you can work in a circular fashion, stitching around the edges of a section, moving towards the center. Remember that you may need to use increases or decreases to finesse the fit of the various beads. Consider leaving a few small, peekaboo voids where you can see through to the central bead's surface.

Don't remove the skewer until you finish the stitching - the beading forms a skin over the base bead, but isn't actually connected to it. This means the beading could rotate and the center hole become lost if the skewer is removed too early.

Design Notes: *Quinacridone Summer*

A process photo from the construction of my *Quinacridone Summer* beaded bead. I'm still using the rattan skewer to keep track of my beading holes.

Working my way around the circle, filling one of the voids in my bead work. This is a different view of the same section from the first photo.

Almost done. I added a line of turquoise accent beads to provide a cool shot of color.

Adding Spikes, Discs and Larger Shaped Beads

Don't limit yourself to traditional seed beads when stitching your beaded beads. Shaped beads add dramatic textural effects. Magatamas can mimic feathers or scales; square Tilas provide a strong geometric element; and spike beads add a dynamic energy like electrons zooming around a molecule, or energy shooting into outer-space. And we are just barely scraping the surface of possible bead choices.

If you plan to use shaped beads, give some thought to their placement before getting started. What is the effect you're trying to achieve? Once you know that, it's easier to use the shaped beads effectively.

Left: Whispers in Pink and Andromeda I by Karen Williams.

Working with Spikes or Accent Beads

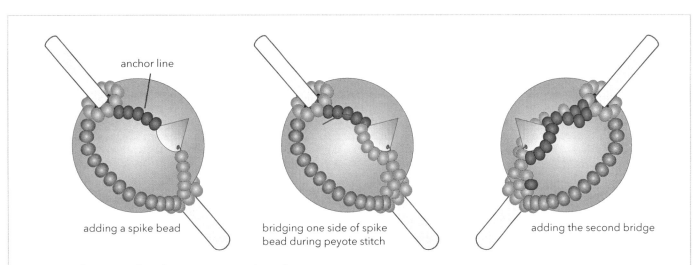

anchor line

adding a spike bead

bridging one side of spike bead during peyote stitch

adding the second bridge

String spikes or other larger accent beads while setting up your initial network of bead strands.

Stitch through the shaped bead or accent bead *at least twice* to fully secure it. Circle each side of the bead as you work peyote stitch along its anchor strand.

Depending upon the diameter of your shaped bead, you may want to work several rows of peyote stitch along the anchor line before circling around the bead. Sometimes you'll have to skip stitches to make everything work, especially in the early stages. You can fill the dents in later with peyote stitch, or use them as pockets for smaller accent beads.

Mixing it Up

Earrings, brooches and pendants are great ways to try mixing freeform peyote with other bead weaving stitches, jewelry techniques and other materials.

Owl Brooch

I received the little owl bead (at left) as part of a Bead Soup Party exchange. He was the cutest little guy, except for the bead hole traveling through his head from side to side. I didn't want it to look like someone had given him a lobotomy, so I decided to create a 'habitat' that would disguise the connection. Using a matte, polished glass ring made from the bottom of a wine bottle (by Cathy Collison of Trinket Foundry) as my background, I added freeform snippets of sky and a beaded branch of cubic right angle weave and freeform peyote for his 'perch'.

Freeform & Wirework

Bobbie Rafferty's simple yet wonderful, free-style earrings combine freeform peyote with brick stitch and wirework.

Earrings and Photography by Bobbie Rafferty of BeadSong Jewelry.

Open Work Earrings

This pair of earrings combines regular right angle weave with freeform peyote, one of my personal favorite bead weaving combinations. The right angle weave (RAW) has a wonderful drape that pairs well with peyote stitch's stiffer structure. RAW also provides easy stitch anchors for peyote stitch borders.

While these earrings are larger than I would normally wear, they are still quite light due to their open, lattice-like design.

I've included a peak into my construction process for both earrings, followed by a quick refresher on basic right angle weave.

Earring One

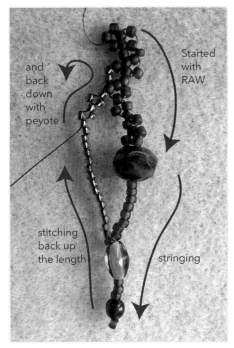

The first earring started with a length of right angle weave, before switching to stringing. Near the top, I anchored into the RAW and started to work back down with peyote stitch.

I worked peyote stitch along the grey-blue line of beads, then stitched through to the bottom, adding a new bridge up to the RAW and then added 6°s to fill the gaps.

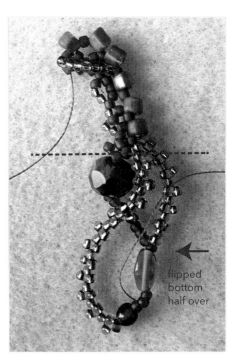

Flipping the bottom half over to create a twist, I peyote stitched down the new bridge, and back up. To finish, I added a blue stabilizing bridge to the left and decorative 8°s.

Earring Two

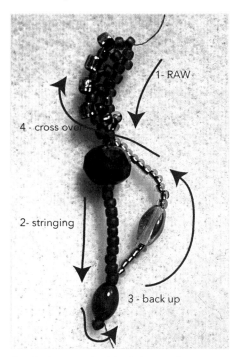

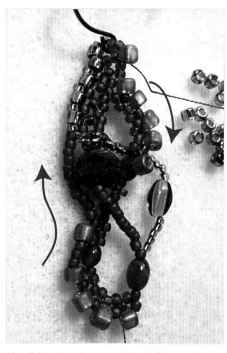

Again I started with right angle weave, then switched to stringing beads. On my way back up, I switched to peyote stitch along the edge of the RAW.

I added a bridge twisting through the first two, attached to the bottom bead, then worked peyote stitch back up along its length.

The blue bridge on the left-hand side helps hold the twist in place. As a finishing touch, I added size 6° beads for accents.

Basic Right Angle Weave

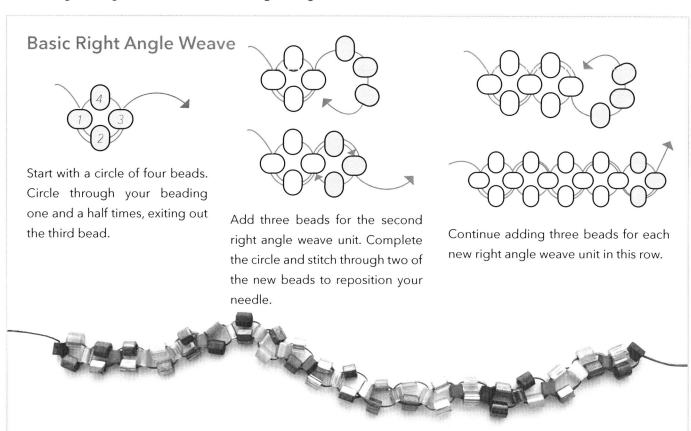

Start with a circle of four beads. Circle through your beading one and a half times, exiting out the third bead.

Add three beads for the second right angle weave unit. Complete the circle and stitch through two of the new beads to reposition your needle.

Continue adding three beads for each new right angle weave unit in this row.

CHAPTER THREE

Working With Ruffles

At their simplest, ruffles occur when there are too many beads, or the beads are too large, for the work to lay flat. Ruffles start out as unseemly bulges and grow into their beauty with a little attention.

Ruffle Sample #1 - As Fast as You Can Go

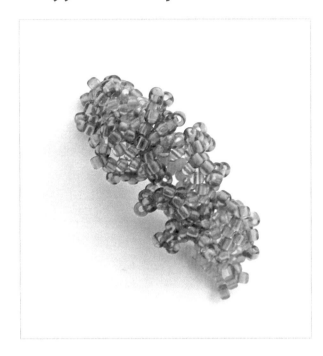

What makes a Ruffle?

Before launching into specific projects using ruffles, I'd like to share the results of a few stitch experiments looking at how different increase patterns affect the look of the finished ruffles. Each of these experiments started with twenty (20) beads and one normal row of peyote stitch. From there, I'll note each variation separately.

Ruffle Experiment #1

Increases every other row

Row 4	increase (add 2 beads) at each opportunity
Row 5	add 1 bead, including between bead pairs
Rows 6-9	repeat steps in rows 4 & 5

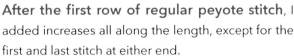

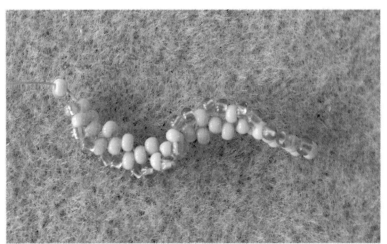

After the first row of regular peyote stitch, I added increases all along the length, except for the first and last stitch at either end.

Note how the beading wants to curve inward as a flat circle. Straighten the line out by tugging on the two beading threads at either end, then use your fingers to gently manipulate the beads into the shape you want.

Tell the Ruffle what you want. As you begin to work the increases, the beads will want to spiral around your center line. Maintain tension and untwist spirals so they form side to side ruffles instead. Manipulate the beading with your fingers until the central rib (the standard peyote stitch edge) lies in one continuous line facing the bottom. Unless, of course, you want your work to spiral - then by all means let the stitching curl as you work.

Row 5: Adding a bead between an increase pair. Add a single bead at each opportunity along the length, including between bead pairs from Row 4.

Full view of Row Five: At this point it looks like a lumpy caterpillar. The ruffle runs along the length in an undulating S-shape.

Row 6: Changing colors to make it easier to see the new increases. Again adding increases all along the length except the first and last stitches.

Full view of Row Six: Still looks rather funny, though the ruffle shape is becoming more distinct. You can easily see the newly added bead pairs.

Row 8: Starting my last row of paired increases (this time in darker blue).

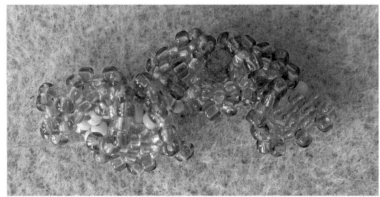

Tight Ruffle: We have ruffles! But see how tight they are - it would be difficult to make them much larger as each ruffle would be squashed by its neighbor.

Ruffle Sample #2 – Looser, Larger Ruffles

The goal with this experiment was to create fewer, but more distinct ruffles that could be built upon beyond the nine rows of stitching of the previous sample.

Ruffle Experiment #2

Increases start with Row 5

Row 5	increase (add 2 beads) at each opportunity
Row 6	add 1 bead, including between bead pairs
Row 7	add 1 bead, regular peyote stitch
Row 8	increase (add 2) at each opportunity
Row 9-10	add 1 bead, including between bead pairs
Row 11	increase (add 2 beads) at each opportunity

halfway through Row 6, working right to left

Row 4: The extra row of regular peyote stitch gives a little extra height without adding bulk to the finished ruffles.

Row 5: I increased all along the length except for the first stitch, which was regular peyote.

Row 6: Switching colors, I added light turquoise beads all along the length, completing the increases.

Choosing your Ruffle Shape - A or B

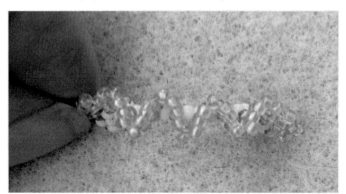

Finishing Row 7: I worked this row in regular peyote stitch. Note that we've nearly doubled the number of beads from the starting row.

Row 7 - Adjusting the Ruffle: It's now time to shape the ruffle, using your fingers to adjust the beading. I decided I preferred three larger ruffles.

Row 8: Using the medium turquoise beads, I added increases all along the length

Rows 9 & 10: by adding two rows of regular peyote between each row of increases, I've reduced the overall number of ruffles. At the same time, it increased the volume of each individual ruffle so its shape is more pronounced.

Row 11: For the last row, I again added two beads at each opportunity, which helped smooth the ruffled edge. Stitching back along this edge again would help to soften it further.

This ruffle is two rows wider than the first experiment. I could have easily added another couple of rows before running out of space between ruffles.

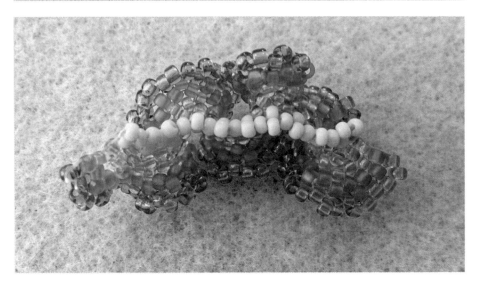

Bottom View: A view of the completed ruffle from underneath. You can see how the initial beading has become a central 'spine' underneath the ruffles.

This view really reminds me of a giant clam!

Ruffle Sample #3 – Shaping the Ruffle

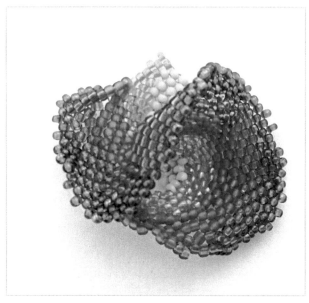

To create larger ruffles, you need to start with a strong foundation of regular peyote stitch, and then be willing to use selective increases as necessary to shape your ruffle.

I usually start with at least five rows of regular peyote stitch for larger, shaped ruffles. I will then add a couple of rows of increases to get the ruffles off to a quick start. With this foundation in place, I manipulate and reshape the ruffle with my fingers until it roughly forms the shape I want.

From there, the key is to add increases only where necessary to keep flaring your desired curve or curves. It is very similar to building a flat curve in that you're looking for a smooth, cone-shaped transition here.

Row 1-5: regular peyote.

Row 6: all increases

Row 7: add 1, including between bead pairs

Row 8: regular peyote

Row 9 and beyond: from here, I started adding increases selectively, only where needed to keep shaping the piece into a large, S-shaped curve.

Keep track of the gaps between beads: wherever the gaps grow too large to fill with a single, I added two. I also added two wherever needed to keep the shape growing.

Comparing the Ruffle Samples

Ruffle Sample #1 - 9 rows

Ruffle Sample #2 - 11 rows

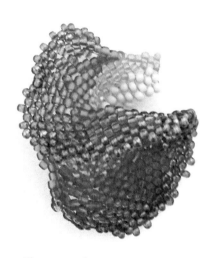

Ruffle Sample #3 ~19 rows

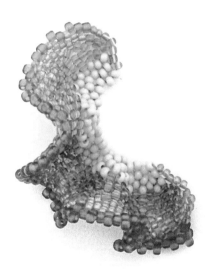

Ruffle Sample #4 ~16 rows

This photo makes it easier to compare the different ruffle stitch samples. The samples are as close to their actual size as possible. Ruffle Sample #1 truly looks like a 'fuzzy caterpillar' when compared to the small, but distinct curves of Ruffle Sample #2.

In contrast, Ruffle Sample #4 (not shown previously) is just getting started. At sixteen rows of stitching, its gentle curves mean that I could build these ruffles up quite a bit before flaring out as in Ruffle Sample #3.

Spiral Dancer Earrings

The pattern for these earrings began as an experiment with the differences between flat spirals and ruffles.

The earring on the right is a modified S-curve (discussed in Chapter 1) and lays relatively flat along a single plane. In contrast, the earring on the left curls into three dimensions.

You can create a mixed pair, or matched sets of either flat or ruffled spiral earrings.

This is a great starting point for additional explorations. The pattern is easily adapted to brooches and pendants. After the design notes, I've included a gallery with several other pieces that started from this same basic pattern. The key is how far you decide to take it.

Row 1-3: String a stop bead, then thirty-six (36) 11° beads. Reverse stitching directions, peyote stitch back along the length.

Row 4: Working along the left edge, add pairs of 11° beads to start the outer curves. Alternate decreases and adding single 11°s to form the interior curves.

Row 5: Repeat along the right edge, following the curves from the previous row. Add pairs of 11°s along outer curves. Alternate decreases and single 11°s along inner curves.

Notes: The bead colors in the diagrams are for illustrative purposes only - the beads along the inner curve should match your base color. Dotted lines and "S"s indicate you should stitch through those areas without adding beads.

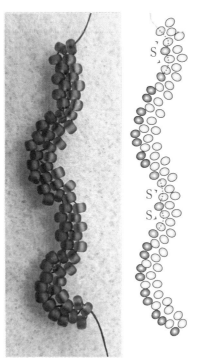

Row 4: photograph and diagram

Row 5: photograph and diagram

Row 7: Peyote stitch along the outside curves along the left edge using 11°s, including between the bead pairs. You may use the same or a different color as the previous row.

Stitch through the inside curves, but don't add any additional beads.

Row 8: Repeat along the other edge. The beads will not lay flat - this is to be expected since we're making ruffles. Watch your thread as it will try to wrap around the new beads because they tend to stick out from the main body.

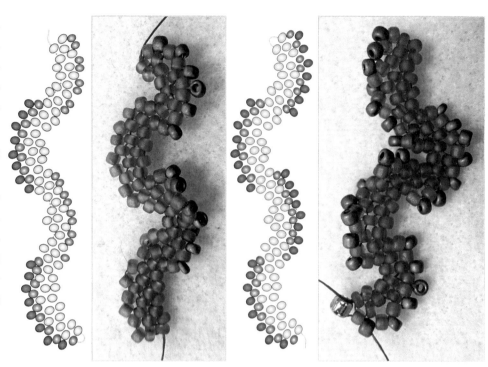

Row 7: photograph and diagram   *Row 8: photograph and diagram*

Row 9 and 10   *Row 11 and 12*

Row 9 & 10: Add single 8° beads between the 11°s from rows seven and eight. The piece will buckle strangely at this point. Spend a little time smoothing the curves to shape them before continuing to stitch.

Rows 11 & 12: Add a single 6° bead between each of the 8°s. String two or three 8°s or 6°s to bridge the gaps between ruffle sections, stitching from side to side and pulling them inward.

Stitch through the outer edge on each side at least twice to secure the larger beads. The curves should smooth out into large ruffles. Because this pattern uses larger beads for the step ups, it works up very quickly. As an alternate, you could use 11°s and increases instead to create a different look.

Add the Earwires: If you're creating earrings, now is the time to add the earwires.

Spiral Dancer Gallery

Pendants, Brooches and Earrings

Each started with the same stitching pattern. With some, I took the ruffles further than others. I often don't know quite what I'm making at first; I might start out planning to make an earring, but it becomes a pendant as I stitch.

Stone Brooch Series

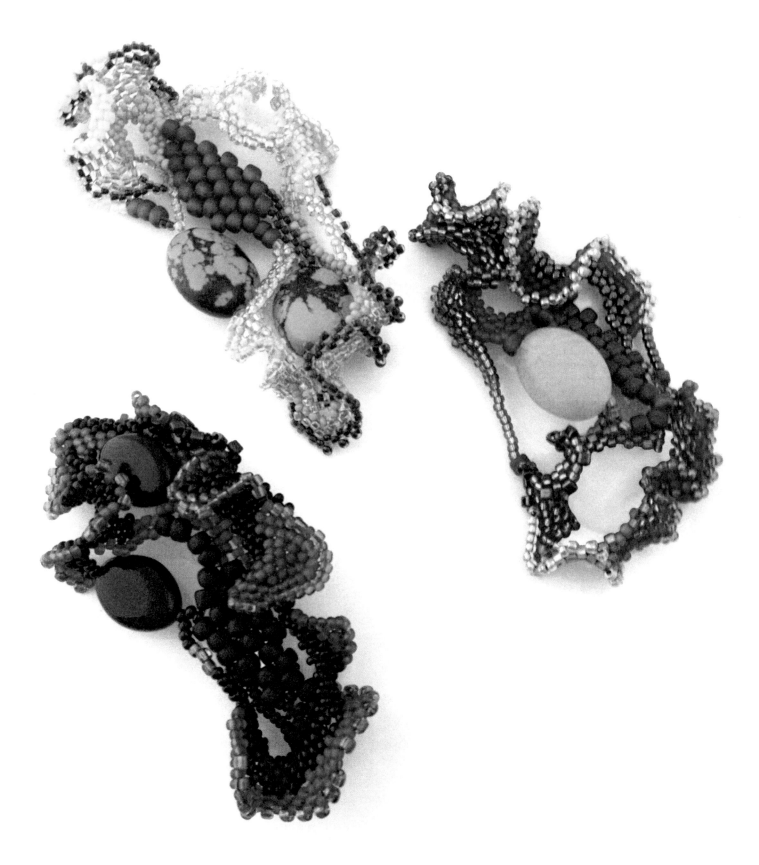

Dragon Thief Brooch

The stone beads reminded me of robin's eggs, so I decided to use a spring theme for the colors in this piece. However, the curled ruffles of the finished piece reminded me more of Chinese dragons than robins, hence the name.

These are more freeform than my Spiral Dancer series.

Constructing the Brooch

Starting with about 48" inches of beading thread, I strung a stop bead, leaving a six to eight inch tail. In my starting length, I included one of my two focal beads, a dyed magnesite puffed oval (~15mm x 20mm).

Beading thread: chartreuse green Superlon AA.

Starting Row Four on the left edge. The whole thing looks pretty awkward at this point. For the next few rows, I simply built on the initial color blocks except at the far left, where I switched to light blue almost immediately.

By about the eighth row, I have added two bridges to encircle my stone focal. I've added a bridge along the top edge of the amethyst 6°s.

At the far right, you can see the squiggly start of my first ruffle.

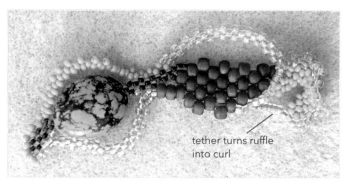

tether turns ruffle into curl

A little further along, I have added a tether, turning the ruffle into a curl and worked peyote stitch along the new bridge.

Time to change threads.

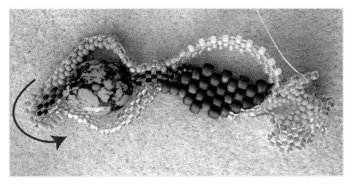

Focusing most of my attention, I worked on the curled ruffle at right.

At the left edge, I've brought the turquoise beads down to curl around the end to outline the soft yellow.

We are still in the ugly duckling stage!

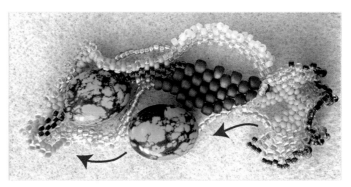

I've added the second magnesite bead to fill an open space in my design. The bridge runs from the inner edge of the blue curl at the right, along the edge of my main line of stitching, through the new focal and under the yellow ruffle at left.

Starting to ruffle with light blue along the top edge.

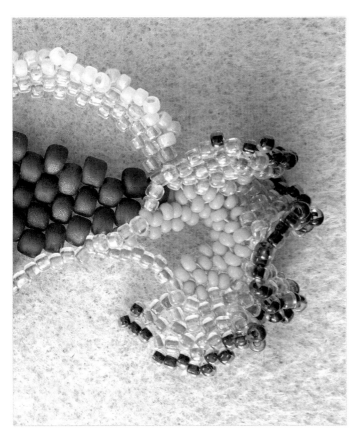

A closeup of the curled ruffle. This is enlarged to 150% of normal size.

I've outlined the ruffle with darker, blue-lined yellow beads. These particular beads remind me of fish eggs. The surprising value contrast helps to keep the brooch from becoming too 'sweet', while the inner color echoes the darker striations in the dyed magnesite.

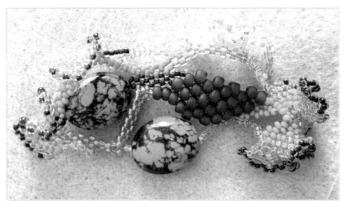

Continuing to build the ruffle along the upper edge. Note that I've carried the yellow over the top now. From a design perspective, it's typically better if each color is echoed at least once in your design.

Almost Done - adding finishing touches to the ruffles. At this point I'm working specific sections to finish melding colors and shape the ruffles.

Poppy Hat Brooch

Enameled poppy discs and custom head pins by artist D. Lynne Bowland.

Inspired by D Lynne Bowland's fiery, enameled poppy-colored discs and head pins, I decided to create a brooch for my favorite sun hat.

Lynne's poppies are so lovely, I wanted my beading to take on a completely supporting roll, so decided to work with a palette of greens and neutral colors. I love the way the poppy's unopened flowers buds twist and curl, so I wanted to try to use that as additional inspiration in my beading.

Selecting my color palette, I first pulled out a number of poppy reds and oranges that matched Lynne's enameled disks as well as a wide range of greens. The red beads seemed to muddy the color scheme.

In the end, I chose greens in a wide range of values. To that, I added a rich, chocolate brown and a couple of soft golds the color of dried grasses.

Auditioning bead palettes. I worked through several possibilities, and finally decided to work with a wide value range of soft greens and some muted golds.

Midway through this project, I needed to stop and figure out where I was going next. Placing my beading onto my sketchbook, I started filling in the 'gaps' with colored pencils.

The photo at left shows my work table as I sketched.

Below are two shots of my sketched background, both with and without the enameled poppies. I later used the second photo as a reference for both beading and poppy placement.

Filling section based upon sketch

starting to ruffle

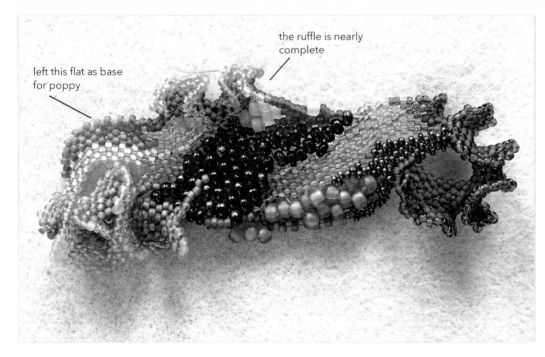

left this flat as base for poppy

the ruffle is nearly complete

Compare these process photos to my sketches on the previous page to see how I translated them into beading.

It is still freeform - I didn't count beads or follow a n actual pattern - the sketch simply gave me a clear idea of how the brooch *could* look.

I like working in threes, so I added a third ruffle along the new edge (similar to Ruffle Sample #2).

Adding the Poppies: Working up from the base, I placed the poppies using my photograph from page 76 as reference.

Just for fun, each poppy has a slightly different center.

Preparing to add the headpins. I considered different ways to incorporate the wires, including drawing them through to the back, creating a little anchor loop, then clipping the wires close to the bead work.

That seemed a waste of good design material, so I decided to wind the copper into another layer of curls, this time floating on the surface.

Curled Head Pins

I used a curved needle to attach the curled head pins. Stitching them in place using One-G beading thread, I hid the stitching under the enameled head. I used the same needle to attach the brooch pin to the back.

I needed very tight curls, so I ended up using a bamboo skewer (same as for my beaded beads) as my center rod. Each end is finished off with a smaller curlicue created using a pair of round nose pliers.

Coral Dancer Bracelet

Inspired by my ongoing love of sea forms including nudibranches, and giant clams, I started this piece intending to create a lariat-style necklace dripping with ruffles. Partway into the project, I realized I would never wear such a necklace.

Unwilling to abandon the beading I had already completed, I decided to convert it into a cuff. Before I could do so, I had to prepare the piece for surgery. First, I determined exactly where it needed to be cut. Before pulling out my scissors, I reinforced the peyote stitch on the 'keeper' side of the incision, much the same way I finish off thread tails before clipping.

Redesign:
Lariat to Bracelet

At right is one of the few photos I have of the originally intended lariat. I cut the beading in the last red section at the top right, just before the purple section. You can see the red underneath the button in the full-length photo of the bracelet below.

Continuing to work, I added a third section of ruffles and built up the support area for my button.

I had a difficult time finding an appropriate button for the closure. None of the metal buttons I had - gold, copper, brass, silver - looked right. I found a simple, vintage Lucite button at Nancy's Sewing Basket, a local couture sewing store. As an alternative, on-line stores like Etsy can be great resources for unique buttons and other findings.

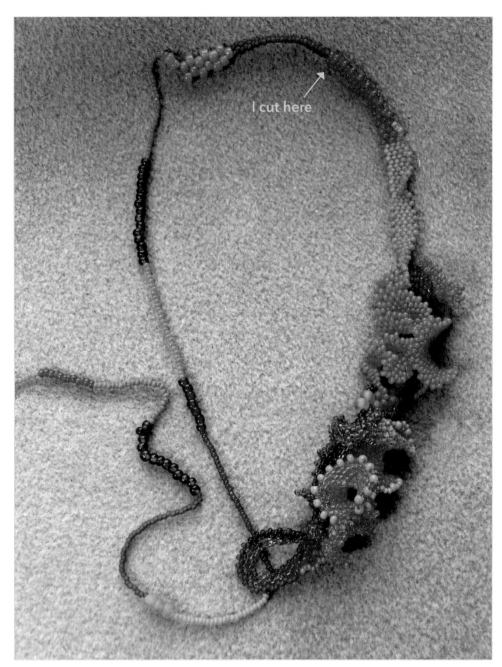

Finished bracelet. The section of red beads under the button is where I cut the piece to form a cuff from the photo above.

Fallen Leaves Cuff

This cuff was inspired by the darker, less intense colors of fallen leaves after they've been dulled by rain and frost, lining the edges of the sidewalk. Meanwhile, the textures remind me of freshly fallen leaves piled high, ruffled by the wind on a crisp autumn day.

I found the limited-edition, Czech beads while planning this piece and had to incorporate them into the design as the colors were perfect and their diamond within a square pattern looked looked like miniature paving stones strewn with autumn leaves.

Row Five(ish): As I've mentioned before, most freeform pieces go through a distinct 'Ugly Duckling' stage. This is especially true for bracelets and cuffs worked along the length, and for this cuff in particular. Here, I've completed about five rows along the main line of stitching, taking a little time out to work on a ruffle near the bead loop. Having one section that looks 'right' so quickly often makes it easier for me to keep stitching. Also note the placement of the Czech beads - they were strung with my first row of beading.

Building up the base before I start adding more ruffles. I stitched several different bead paths through the central section of the cuff, all ready for further development. The cuff is quite crooked at this point; this is alright.

Focusing on ruffles along the lower edge of the piece. I changed colors and defined separate starting and ending points every two to three inches (2-3") along the length. This makes the beading stand out as several distinct ruffles instead of one continuous line. I preferred this more layered effect as it better fit my theme.

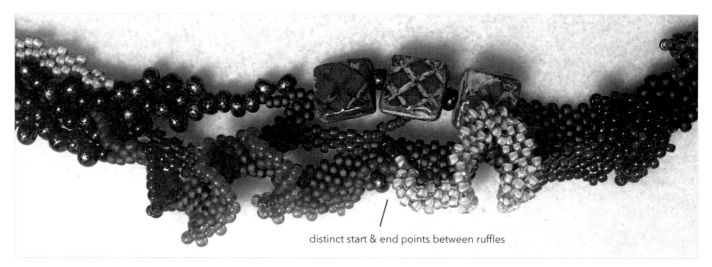

distinct start & end points between ruffles

A close-up of the ruffles along the lower edge. They are just a little further along than in the last photo, but their distinctive forms are starting to take shape. The flat upper edge of the cuff still looks quite awkward; it will definitely need some attention. I want to frame the Czech glass beads instead of allowing them to float atop the design.

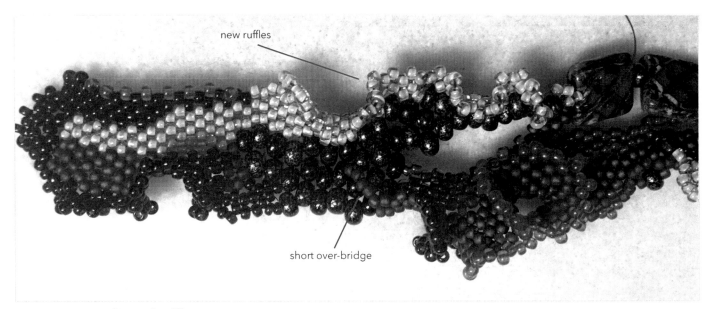

new ruffles

short over-bridge

Starting a new line of ruffles along the upper left. I decided to draw the creamy tan beads further towards the center of the design, so they seem to disappear into the 'paving stone' Czech beads and then reappear below.

Ruffling so close to where I plan to place my button, I had to check periodically to make sure there was still enough space for my button to lay flat.

Also, note how I used a short over-bridge to draw the edge of the bottom ruffle into the darker beads.

Almost done, except the Czech beads still seem to float above the rest of the piece. I needed to add a little something more to their right to help integrate them more fully into the design.

I could have stopped here, and the piece would have been all right. Instead this is the point where I go into 'trouble shooting' mode, looking for weak areas of the design and ways to balance out my beading. As I work, I look at the cuff both flat and wrapped around my wrist.

Tip: It is important to try your work on periodically to see how it looks when worn since that is how it will primarily be seen in its completed form.

A close-up view of the bracelet's under side. For additional support, I ran a series of short bridges under each of the Czech beads, tying them more firmly into the bracelet. You can also see evidence of my thread changes in the chocolate beads at the far left. I try to work my thread changes from the bottom to hide any ugliness they may cause.

Adding the Button

I'd planned to use a ceramic leaf button for my closure, but its color (bottom far left) was too bright and fresh for the finished bracelet.

Since I had several buttons to play with, I pulled out my alcohol inks and altered the colors - shading one more towards green and another towards burgundy.

Buttons receive more wear and handling than purely decorative elements, and I'm uncertain how well the alcohol inks will wear over time. For this reason, I would not use an ink-colored button for a piece I planned to sell.

Jennifer Porter

FEATURED ARTIST

Jennifer draws her inspiration from walking and kayaking through the wild spaces around the Seattle area where she makes her home, and from her frequent visits to Hawaii, the home of her heart.

Starting with a Peyote Stitch Base

When creating bracelets, Jennifer often starts by stitching a simple peyote stitched base using size 8°s or 6°s. The larger beads work up quickly and are easier to stitch into than 11°s. In the end, the base band is almost completely hidden beneath her elaborate embellishments of ruffles and fringe.

In her *Ocean Deep* bracelet, Jennifer started with a band of 6°s in iridescent blues. She stitched the band lengthwise rather than from side to side as this provided easier anchor points for her later embellishments.

From there, she worked a line of freeform ruffles off of both edges. Filling in the center with additional ruffles, as well as leaf and seaweed style fringe, Jennifer finished off the bracelet with a shell and pearl focal that also doubles as her button closure.

Jennifer prefers Sono nylon beading thread, which is relatively strong, and easy to thread on a needle. For fishing line type thread, she prefers Power Pro. She feels it has wonderful flexibility, and is well suited to her slightly looser, flowing style.

Facing page: Ocean Deep by Jennifer Porter. Above right: view of the base band from the underside with 10 rows of size 6° seed beads.

Quick Seaweed Fringe

String beads the desired length of your fringe. Reversing directions, stitch back through the second to last bead (hereafter called the turn bead).

Fringe Branches: Stitch up through several beads along the main strand. Come out and string 4-7 beads. Reversing directions, stitch back through the turn bead to the main strand.

Add as many fringe branches as you'd like, working back up the main strand to the top. Stitch through everything twice.

Untitled Bracelet by Jennifer Porter. Inspired by the colors of Seattle's wild spaces, and more specfically the colors of pond scum in late winter. Who knew pond scum could be so beautiful?

88

Looking beyond the obvious, Jennifer is drawn to the textures, shapes, and fantastic color combinations that are found in the least likely places. Speaking with her, she explained, "I am moved, for example, by the rich colors found in pond scum, goose poop, and yard waste, when the light hits it just right!"

When asked to describe her creative process, she replied "My creative process is based on the fact that I cannot follow a recipe. I have to make things unique or it's somehow not worth doing, for me."

Introduced to freeform peyote while taking a beading class at Ocean Sky bead shop in Carlsbad, CA, she was immediately drawn to the medium. A later class on freeform peyote ruffles at Fusion Beads in Seattle opened another world of options. She likes to study new techniques and stitches so she can "deviate intelligently." In her current work, Jennifer often combines multiple stitches, including freeform peyote, freeform netting stitches, random right angle weave, and herringbone stitch. Her favorite thing to do is pick up a needle and thread and start doodling with beads!

Jennifer's ruffles are much softer, with looser tension than mine, giving her pieces a lovely, fabric-like drape.

This bracelet was part of a series called "Slough Bling," inspired by winter kayaking trips in the Seattle area. Jennifer worked freeform peyote ruffles and leaf fringe over a peyote stitch base of size 6° seed beads. Right: an inspiration photo shot from her kayak while on the Sammamish Slough.

CHAPTER FOUR
Designing Larger Jewelry Projects

Freeform Bracelets - Stages of Work

Bracelets and cuffs seem to be the singular most popular item made in freeform peyote, for good reasons. Large enough to truly experiment with the medium; they are challenging but surprisingly forgiving, and quite frankly, they're loads of fun to wear. While I touched on bracelets in the last chapter, we will start this chapter by looking at the stages of design and creation.

* **Stitch the Base Structure** - don't worry if it doesn't stay a perfectly straight line. Bracelets are very forgiving and straight borders aren't required in order for the finished piece to look great around your wrist.

* **Decorate the Surface** - it's easiest to add fringe, extra bridges across the top, and other such items after you've completed the main body of your bracelet. Such items tend to act as thread magnets, catching and tangling your beading thread with each stitch. It's also easier to position them accurately once your base is complete.

* **Attach the clasp, button or findings** - save the clasp for last for the same reasons I listed above. Then, as soon as it's in place, your bracelet is ready to wear.

'Atlantis Found' bracelet by Sherry Eagle. Take a closer look at the way she's combined a wide range of beads, few of which are size 11° seed beads, and at the shaping details she added to the two ends. Photography by artist.

Demeter's Harvest Bracelet

The beauty of the winter landscape is more subtle than that of the warmer seasons. The colors and lines reflect an understated elegance in a symphony of umber, sienna, golds, creams and frost-tinged blues.

In *Demeter's Harvest*, I sought to celebrate this quieter season.

Chinese crystals and glass pearls from ZnetShows were the starting point for this design. From there, I added an assortment of seed beads, including twin-hole SuperDuos Czech beads.

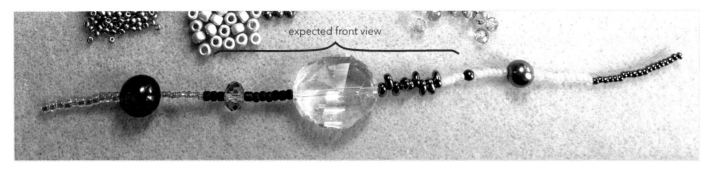

The Starting Row. Because I always think of the closure side of a bracelet as an alternate front, I added a 12mm pearl towards the left edge. This time around, I chose not to include a button loop as part of my starting row.

Row Four, starting Row Five at far left. For this piece, I decided to use 4lb crystal Fireline because I didn't want any thread color to show through the clear crystal focal. I've worked bridges around the 8mm pearl and the central crystal. Alternating SuperDuos and size 11° seed beads created a nice fan effect around my crystal focal.

Decided to add a button loop. Normally I add my button loop with my starting row. Here, I've completed approximately six rows on the left hand side. On the right, the bracelet is up to about nine rows. Working with the SuperDuos beads, I found you have to think more about thread paths, because it's much harder to change stitching directions than with regular seed beads. Up to this point, my goal was to build organically shaped blocks of color.

moving light blue

continuing to build this edge

outlined cream with bronze

filled in this area

moving gold, new 12mm pearl

new patch of blue

Leaving the Ugly Duckling Stage This bracelet is just starting to emerge from its Ugly Duckling stage; we can now catch a glimpse of its completed form. Working a section at a time, I've continued building around the edges, moving colors and textures to improve flow and contrast. Rather than a solid bead loop, I decided to work a series of arching bridges around its outer edge for a lacier look.

more SuperDuos

double row of arching bridges

Left: I added a second layer of lacy bridges around the bead loop, working with 11° Charlottes. Along the lower edge, I extended the bronze and gold beads to provide extra definition. Along the top edge I've added a little patch of SuperDuos that will need to be more fully worked into the design before I'm done.

Below Left: I've widened the right end of the bracelet to support the crystal toggle I plan to add. I kept the end fairly simple as it will be mostly hidden when worn, but couldn't resist adding a single crystal. After all, the wearer will see that end when they take the bracelet on and off. I want it to be pretty too!

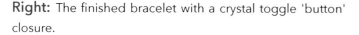

attached crystal toggle here

Right: The finished bracelet with a crystal toggle 'button' closure.

To attach the toggle, I stitched up from the bracelet and strung a line of three seed beads, the crystal, an O-bead, and a small gold 11° seed bead for the turn bead. While quite secure, the crystal can move about on its tether when the bracelet is fastened, giving it a more dynamic finish than a regular button.

95

Nautilus Flower Cuff

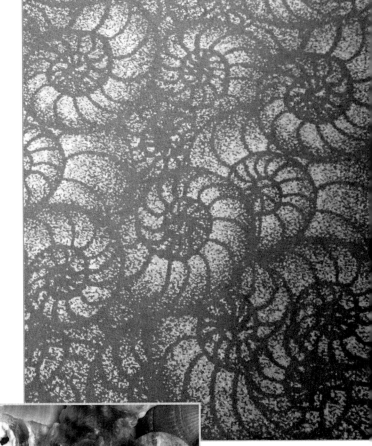

This bracelet began as a series of questions. What would happen if I borrowed my color palette from sea shells, but played with the color balance? What if, in my design the pinks and purples dominated over the creamy whites? How could I translate the feel of a pile of sea shells, all overlapping and jumbled into a bracelet? What would the finished design look like?

Different than I originally imagined, but it could look a lot like my Nautilus Flower cuff. One of the last pieces created for this book, I packed the beads for this bracelet planning to work on it while on a transatlantic cruise. On my first day on the ship, I stumbled upon this carpet (photography at right) in one of the ship's public areas. An almost a perfect match both in terms of colors and interpretation of my original inspiration, I couldn't stop smiling at the similarities and had to take a picture.

Above: a carpet aboard the Disney Magic.

Left: sea shells for color palette. I decided to use far more of the purples.

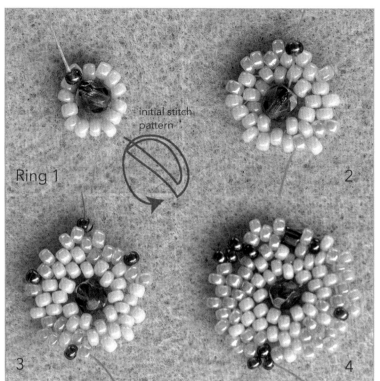

Ring 1

initial stitch pattern

2

3

4

Building Circles

I started by stitching several circles, as follows.

Ring 1: I strung a stop bead, a 4mm fire-polished bead and enough 11° seed beads to circle one half of the fire-polished bead. I stitched through all of the beads twice before completing the outer ring with more beads.

Ring 2 and beyond: From there, I began to peyote stitched around the ring. Whether I started the increases in this ring or the next varied from circle to circle, as did the exact placement of the increases. In the sample at left, increased in the second ring.

Building the circles, I used increases as necessary to keep the beading flat, but played with the designs as I went. I also created several circle starts (2-3 rings) before beginning construction of the cuff.

Connecting Circles

A

B

Building off of the circle start

Once I had a collection of circles, I began joining them, edge to edge. To create the feel of overlapping edges, I stitched some circle starts to the edges of completed circles, as shown in the insert above (A), then continued building off of the now connected circle starts (B).

Elsewhere, I started new circles stitching between the edges of connected circles (C). Where the space was too tight to fit one of my circle starts, this proved to be the best solution.

C

starting a new circle

D

building circle

Playing with potential layouts for my pansy shells. I stitched several extra whole pansy shells, then played with different ways that I might combine them with my starting section.

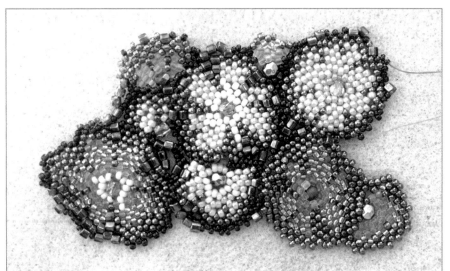

Stitching new pansy shells into place. I've added one of my whole pansies and a couple of pansy halves along the upper edge.

It is at about this point that I decided all of my new pansies should be outlined in the darkest purple as I liked the lines and sense of shadow.

I had not decided on a front or back side yet, so the photos flip back and forth along with my focus as I worked on the piece.

Checking the Edge. Working on the circles, it can be difficult to keep a semi-uniform edge. I cut a paper guide 2½" wide to help corral my edges. The bracelet is already wider than what I'd intended, but the width gives me more room to work.

Adding the 'Button' Closure

Planning this cuff, I purchased a collection of Debbie Sanders' lampworked glass discs. I thought to add a layer of the discs scattered across the top of my bead work as another layer of design. As the cuff developed, I found I didn't want to hide my beading.

In the end, I used a single disc as the 'button' for my closure. To make it work as a button, I stitched one last pansy shell using a 4mm fire-polished center and 15° seed beads. I placed the disc along the border between two pansy shells.

For my button loop, I used the same colors as in the pansy shells, radiating out from the center. If I were to change one thing about this design, I might add a series of circles on either side of the loop to help integrate it into the design, but I think that it works well enough as it is, especially once the cuff is buttoned.

Natalia Malysheva
FEATURED ARTIST

Like most artists drawn to freeform peyote, Natalia loves to experiment, asking the question "what if", then working out her answers as she stitches. Natalia draws her inspiration from her total environment; the sounds, the smells, the landscape, water ... music ... art. Anything she sees, hears or experiences is fair game for artistic interpretation. Sometimes inspiration comes to her in a dream - she keeps a journal handy to sketch or write them down before they "melt away" upon waking.

Natalia is also inspired by the work of other artists', which can lead her to try a new-to-her bead weaving technique, a different way of combining stitches, to experiment with color combinations outside of her usual palettes, or to work with different kinds of materials. She suggests that the key to using other artists' work as inspiration is to pull individual ideas from the whole, then find ways to reinterpret those ideas as your own. Rather than saying "I want to make that piece", instead ask "what would happen if I worked with similar colors?" or "how could I use jasper in my work?". Then play with your answers to see where they might lead.

When asked how she chooses her color palettes, Natalia explained that often the choice of color is almost accidental. For example, she might scatter and mix a few bags of beads, creating a beautiful "bead-soup" combination. Her palettes are also inspired by nature - blooming Estonian fields and deep forests. After that, all that remains is to weave it all together.

Natalia prefers to work with Czech and Japanese beads because she likes the diversity in color, shape and texture. As she notes, "There are smooth beads, matte, transparent, round, square and lots more!" Natalia is particularly fond of matte beads, sea glass and gemstone crystals. She also likes to use the chips of different gemstones, describing their organic shapes as "little pieces of nature around us." Bright coral rounds, stone, polymer clay or even wooden accent beads add subtle contrast to her designs.

Facing page and above: Untitled freeform cuff by Natalia Malysheva. Photography by artist.

Natalia shared several photos of the construction process for this freeform cuff, inspired by the colors of the deep Estonian forests,

Right: close-up of the finished clasp.
Below: Natalia's beading mat and starting length for this bracelet.
All photography on both pages by artist.

Working on Row Four. Natalia hasn't started moving colors yet, but is still building on her original blocks of color.

Further along, she has begun moving colors and added several round, jasper beads. She has also introduced lighter colored, transparent, amber-brown 11°s seed beads. The two ends are now their final widths, although she continued to build the central width her piece.

Attaching the Clasp with Copper Jump Rings

Natalia uses store bought jewelry clasps for most of her bracelets and shared her method for attaching them to her finished work.

Natalia started by attaching three jump rings between the 11° beads at each end of her bracelet.

The three jump rings, attached and closed. Note how they are anchored between the first and second beads.

Attaching a fourth jump ring to her clasp, Natalia then joined the bracelet to the clasp with a fifth jump ring.

Natalia worked this bracelet along its width, creating a very different look from her two previous bracelets, which were both worked along their length.

Working along the width allowed Natalia to create some wonderfully unusual effects, including the vertical 'windows' and the stacked bridges of bugle beads worked in peyote stitch.

The bracelet echoes the lines and textures of the background in her inspiration photograph of the forest floor.

She could have included the purples of the flowers, but they truly weren't necessary and might have even detracted from the softly rich colors of the design. Perhaps purple might make it into her next design.

Again note how she used jump rings to attach the jewelry findings and lobster claw clasp.

All photography by artist.

Surf Necklace by Cynthia Machata

Not all projects go exactly according to plan. Here, Cynthia Machata shares the convoluted design path her *Surf* necklace took on its way to completion. The necklace began with the purchase of 'some wonderful glass' from Fern Hill Glass while visiting family in Astoria, Oregon. A local glass blowing studio, they sell the leftover pieces from their work as sort of rough cabochons.

She began by bezeling the glass cabochons with the brick stitch. Using the cabochons as her starting point, Cynthia then worked outward with freeform peyote and random right angle weave until she reached the point in the middle photo at right.

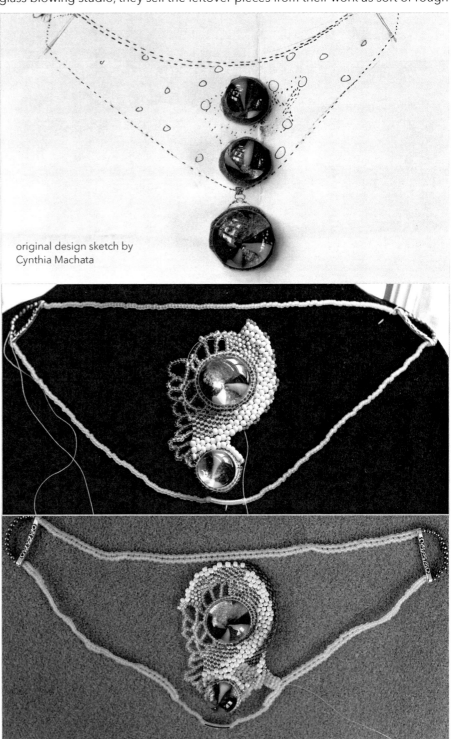

original design sketch by
Cynthia Machata

Design Idea #1

Cynthia planned to stitch her freeform beading into an outlined collar of brick stitch (lower right photo). She decided the piece needed more flow than the border would allow. Removing her work from the border, she returned to her drawing board.

Design Idea #2

Freeing her central design from its collar outline, Cynthia continued to stitch, building a green wave along the right edge. She added a little random right angle weave to give the density of the pattern a bit of breathing room.

Planning an alternate design for the necklace, Cynthia decided to link four copper rings with freeform peyote. This new design would sit at the collar-bone level. As the first step towards her new design, Cynthia covered two of the copper rings in beading using regular right angle weave, a stitch which offers easy anchor points for later bead weaving.

Right: freeform focal with four brass rings for scale.

Below left: her new design sketch.

Below right: covering a brass ring in right angle weave.

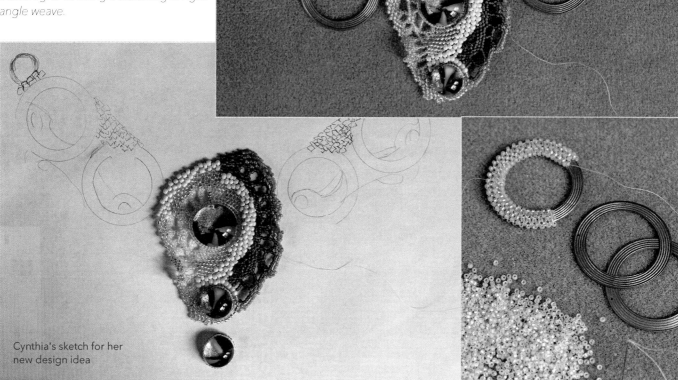

Cynthia's sketch for her new design idea

Design Idea #2b

Connecting her freeform peyote to two bead-covered rings, Cynthia added new lines of freeform beading. The green helps maintain both the color balance and the asymmetry of her design. Deciding the rings overwhelmed the design, Cynthia ripped them back out.

Final Design

In her final design, Cynthia used braid sari silk for the neck bands; they felt more freeform and nautical. At the back she sewed the braid flat so it would hold still in the crimp, then added a magnetic closure.

Below: The side view below showcases the dimensionality of Cynthia's finished necklace. The glass cabochons rest above the general beading like bubbles, while the edging ripples like foam in the surf.

Random Right Angle Weave

Start with a circle of 5 or more beads

String several beads and circle back

String several beads and circle back through both circles

Continue adding beads, stitching back through previous circles

Varying bead numbers increases random appearance

Build each new loop of random RAW by picking up 5-10 beads and circling back through previous loops

All photography on pages 105-109 by Cynthia Machata.

Starfish Bracelet

Once again drawing her inspiration from the sea, this time Cynthia looked to the skeletons of sea stars. This bracelet combines brick stitch and freeform peyote.

She started by connecting the cultured sea glass beads into a chain with brick stitch. Using freeform peyote, Cynthia then surrounded and captured each piece of glass, allowing the freeform beading to partially obscure and soften her brick stitch.

In some places, the brick stitch nearly disappears. Elsewhere it adds an interesting geometry. She finished her bracelet with a handmade copper clasp.

connecting the sea glass with brick stitch

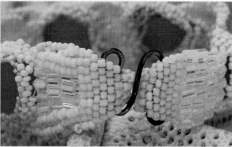

Far left: Cynthia has just started adding freeform peyote to the sea glass furthest to the far right.

Left: a closeup view of the closed copper clasp.

Below: the full bracelet.

Rattlesnake Choker

Originally conceived as a coordinating piece for my *Leopard Jasper* bracelet (featured in my original book), this choker languished for several years in my UFO (unfinished object) pile. I dug it back out after signing up for Sally Russick's *One Crayon Color* challenge and blog hop and choosing to work with the color brown.

Despite my earlier difficulties with the piece, this time around it quickly took on a life of its own. Setting aside my earlier ideas, I let the piece have its way.

This is the point where I had abandoned the piece to my UFO pile. The jasper bead was supposed to be the center front of a traditional choker, but it was too long. Still firmly in its Ugly Duckling stage, I'd lost interest and set it aside.

Focusing on one section at a time

Left: Picking it back up almost a year later, I began building on the existing blocks of color, interspersing additional round jasper accent beads as I went.

Because of its length, I focused on three to five inch (3-5") sections at a time, building each before moving to a new area. Look closely and you'll see both ends of the piece in this photo are still quite narrow.

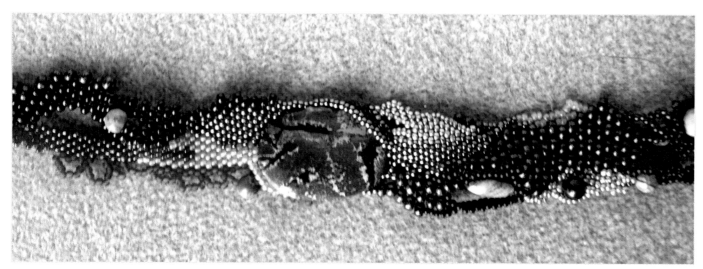

Continuing to work one section at a time, my goal was to build a 'ribbon' of bead work about the same width as the height of the jasper focal. Focusing on the section to the right of the stone, I stitched several new areas of color, adding smaller, jasper accent beads.

Kerchief Choker with Button Focus

Deciding to run with a desert Southwest theme, I changed the design from a traditional choker to one with a 'kerchief' finish (making use of the excess length). The muted color palette and textures reminded me of a snake's skin, particularly the Diamondback Rattlesnake. The triangular shape of the kerchief end strengthened this association further; its elongated diamond like the head of a snake.

The shank on the button I'd originally selected had broken during its time in the UFO bin, so I had to find a replacement. Looking at several options, I found it interesting how dramatically each changed the feel of the piece. In the end, I selected one of the buttons at the top - I liked how it fit into the desert Southwest theme.

The jasper stone now rides center back, but it can also be worn center front, with the kerchief end tucked out of the way.

The Danger Zone Necklace

Sketching and Mock-ups

This necklace started with the lampworked focal bead by JJ Jacobs. I loved the vibrant yellow, and the curved black paths. The black ribbons reminded me of a highway - new black top in the desert - while the colors spoke of caution signs. I decided to leave its yellow as a single point of caution and use the blue and red as accents, with black as my dominant color.

I wanted the piece to be open and a little lacy, with strong sinuous lines.

To help visualize how I wanted it all to come together, I pulled out my sketchbook. Starting with a pencil outline of my paper templates, I used brush-tipped markers to sketch interconnecting ribbons of color. My goal was to draw the blue and red through the piece, appearing and disappearing.

A

B

C

Stitching the Necklace in Sections

Photo A) I added the second red lampworked bead (also by JJ Jacobs) above the focal, along with three separate lines of beading that all connect to a single 6° turn bead.

Photo B) The three lines of beading from photo A are now fully incorporated into the freeform peyote, with additional lines of beading above and to the right.

The scattered blue seed beads along the right edge in (A) are now part of the bold, blue ribbon stretching to the top of photo B.

Photo C) I compared my beading to my drawing to check how things are progressing. Since I created a full-sized sketch of the design, this is a quick way to direct my stitching.

Now it's time to start building towards the right side of the necklace.

A new start. I started on a new section to the right with a single line of beading. Using my peyote stitch to change directions, I stitched back towards the main body of beading.

Filling in the shape with peyote stitch - it reminds me of a stop sign or an 80's video game animation. It's too geometric right now, but I will soften that as I continue to stitch.

Adding new connections - I added a double line of 11° triangles and a ribbon of red and black seed beads. Both snake upwards from below. Also note I've added a second blue accent bead into a circular bridge of seed beads.

Continuing to the right, I added a new line of transparent red 11ºs, then built off of that with peyote stitch.

I am also shaping the very bottom into more of a point, giving it more definition with an extra line of beading.

Shaping the Design

Interconnected lines help shape and anchor each other in place. I'm not trying to do everything at once, but continuing to build curves off of curves, using turn beads to tie off 'loose ends' until I'm ready to take them further.

Above: The new line of red seed beads is now a freeform ribbon outlined with black along its upper edge. Along the bottom edge of the design, I've added the fourth blue accent bead, using a turn bead to finish off that line for now.

The right edge of my black & red 'stop-sign' shape is still too geometric - I'll need to soften that.

Right: All five blue accent beads are in place along the lower left and I'm starting to work up into the neckband.

I don't have to turn every line of beading into peyote stitch - some may remain as they are for contrast.

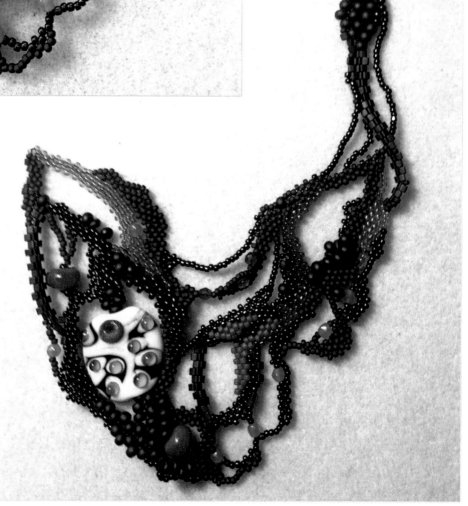

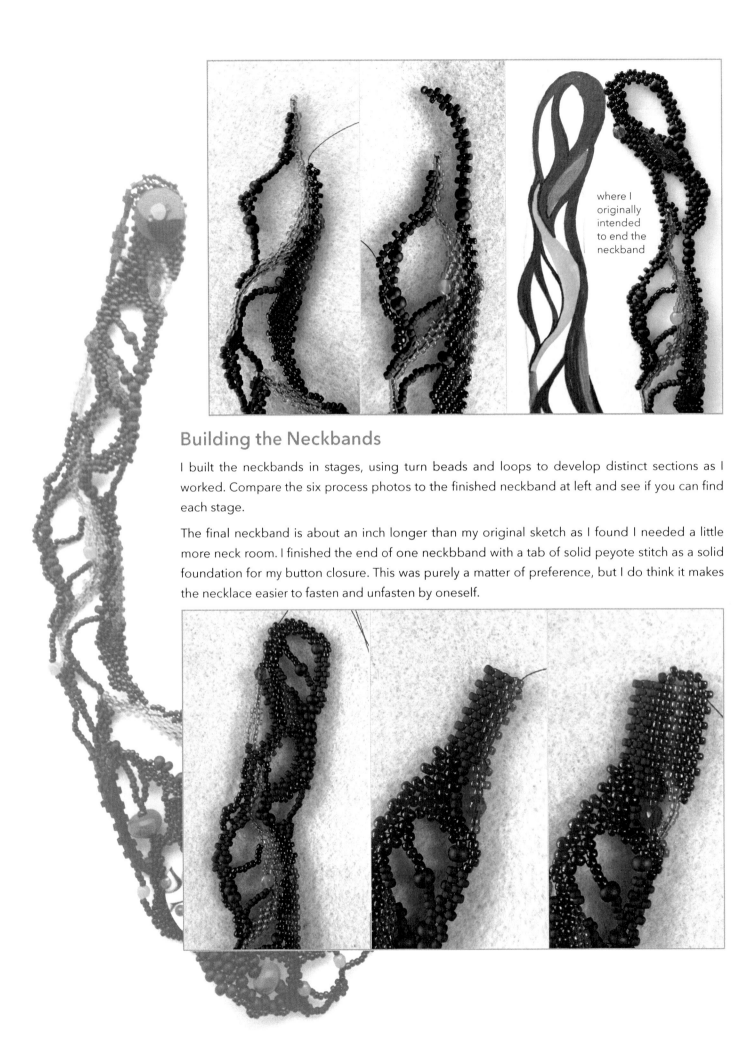

where I
originally
intended
to end the
neckband

Building the Neckbands

I built the neckbands in stages, using turn beads and loops to develop distinct sections as I worked. Compare the six process photos to the finished neckband at left and see if you can find each stage.

The final neckband is about an inch longer than my original sketch as I found I needed a little more neck room. I finished the end of one neckbband with a tab of solid peyote stitch as a solid foundation for my button closure. This was purely a matter of preference, but I do think it makes the necklace easier to fasten and unfasten by oneself.

Opal Essence Necklace

Opal Essence began with a beautiful, fused glass cabochon, also from artist JJ Jacobs. A soft, peachy rose, the cabochon was lit from within with flashes of metallic golds, bronze, iridescent greens and soft blues. I wanted to set it in an equally soft, romantic necklace with a Victorian flare.

Bezeling Focal and Accent Beads

Step 2: I stitched back through my focal and the seed beads from the first side before stringing seed beads around the second side, completing the circle. Then stitched through a few more beads before starting peyote stitch.

Step 1: When bezeling accent beads, I start by stringing a stop bead, stitch through my crystal or focal bead, then string enough beads (usually 11°s) to reach the other side of the focal as in photo A.

Step 3: Peyote stitch along the edge, keeping your tension tight. Transition to smaller (15°) beads to cup the bezel.

Constructing the Necklace

I bezeled JJ's cabochon using a combination of right angle weave and peyote stitch, because the combination drapes easily over irregular shapes and gives me easy anchor points for later stitching.

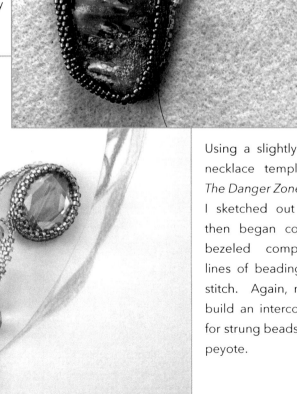

Using a slightly wider paper necklace template than for *The Danger Zone* as my guide, I sketched out some ideas, then began connecting the bezeled components with lines of beading and peyote stitch. Again, my plan is to build an interconnected web for strung beads and freeform peyote.

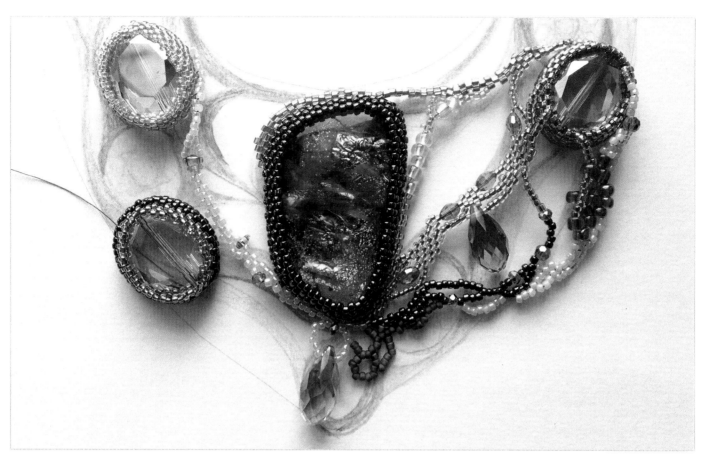

Comparing my work to my colored pencil sketch, I've added two drop crystals to my open web of freeform peyote. The lower drop crystal fills in the central point. I am now ready to start work on the second side of the necklace.

Design Notes: constructing the left side of the necklace front

This series of photographs gives a more detailed look at how I constructed the second side of my necklace front. Take a look at how I added, then built upon the individual lines of beading.

new lines with light green

added a smaller bezeled crystal

antique bronze seed beads form a second connection between crystals

new line with 2 rice-cut crytals

building on that line

adding a drop crystal

Design Notes: building the neckband

With the center front complete, I began work on the neckbands. The insert shows how I built upon earlier stitching.

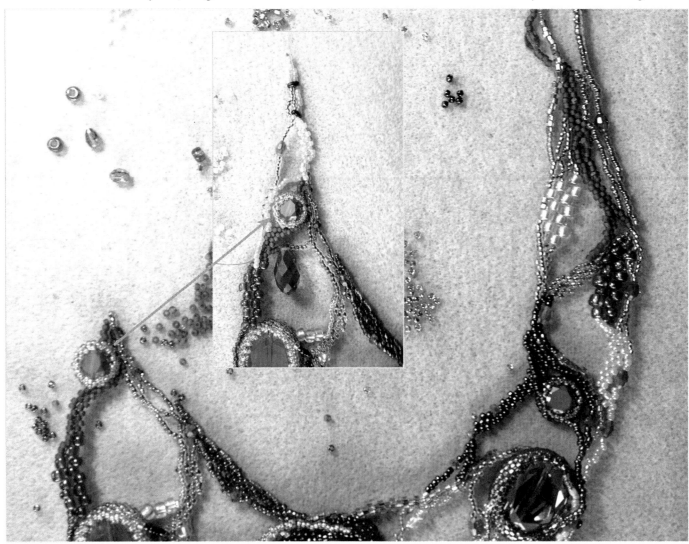

Wendy Hatton

FEATURED ARTIST

Homage to Amphritite Necklace

Walking the beach, collecting little treasures from the tide line, Wendy's imagination conjured pictures of her finds as little beaded creations which could be combined into a freeform necklace. Later, as she worked on the piece, she found herself thinking of Amphritite, the mythological wife of Poseidon, and the queen of the sea.

Wendy imagined Amphritite basking in the sunshine on water-splashed rocks and shimmering with these little treasures from the sea. Drawing on this inspiration, she focused on the organic nature of the shapes. With her stitching, she created reflections of the little nooks and crannies, rock pools and endless beautiful bits and pieces washed upon the shore of her imagination. This necklace is Amphritite's (and Wendy's) garland of sea jewels.

Previous page and above: Homage to Amphritite by Wendy Hatton.
All photography on pages 123-127 by artist.

Wendy began work by gathering her stash, including crystals, pearls, cubes and various sizes of seed beads in golden colors, lining them all up in front of her.

Beginning to stitch, she started by making a number of little organic shapes with these beads. Her hands seemed to gravitate to the beads she needed as she worked. Rather than planning or sketching anything at this stage, she simply allowed the shapes to develop as they would.

Once she had a collection of these beaded 'jewels', Wendy began connecting them together with more freeform peyote and fringing techniques. She describes most of the work as 'totally unconscious' in its conception.

Photo Details

Facing page: Detail of Wendy's collar - see if you can identify some of her starting organic shapes and how she used freeform beading to join them together.

Above: A close-up of a pearl cluster, surrounded by organic waves of freeform peyote seed beads in several sizes. The line of lightly ruffled peyote stitch along the left edge adds to the necklace's organic, design reminiscent of sea wrack tossed onto the shore by high tides.

Right: Several waves of elaborate seaweed fringe cascade from the main body of the necklace, softening and defining its lower edge. Wendy deftly blends more substantial, peyote-stitch ruffled waves with the open fringe. Large pearls and crystal accent beads help give her fringe a very different look.

Amphritite's Golden Cuff & Earrings

This cuff and the earrings on the following page are beautiful examples of working in a series. After completing her *Homage to Amphritite* necklace, Wendy designed this coordinating bracelet and the lovely pair of earrings shown larger than life on the facing page.

Her beaded bauble earrings give us a glimpse at the 'little organic shapes' which helped form the accents for Homage.

Wendy finds the hypnotic and meditative process of handling and creating with beads to be wonderfully satisfying. She states that "When I'm working, I am constantly visualizing images of where my design process is taking me. Often, I recall details that I may have seen in nature or elsewhere which enables the work to flow. However, often the work for me is totally intuitive. I find the design process to be the truly great thing about beading."

"Working freeform gives me total license to let the beads and design evolve and take on a shape of their own. The beads have a very free spirit which we try to contain. I like to just let them work their own 'magic'. I find the 'play of the beads' to be totally different from any other art form I practice."

Wendy takes her beading most places with her, stating "I always have a kit of scissors, needles, thread and numerous seed beads so I can just pick up and bead as I go. Or if I have a project in mind I will take enough of the different beads that I might need to start something or to continue to work on something that I've started. I always seem to take far too much. I am influenced greatly by my surroundings, especially if I'm at the beach."

All photography on both pages by artist.

Janice Cuozzo

FEATURED ARTIST

Sea Delight Necklace

Janice's necklace was inspired by a bead challenge to create a piece that would make a mermaid feel pretty so that her "good side" would win over her "bad side". The accompanying kit included several strands of dyed bamboo coral in red, orange, lime green and cream. Janice immediately knew she would use free form peyote for this creation, adding sand dollars, shells, dagger beads and a variety of seed beads from her stash to "really make this piece a lot of fun."

She starts each necklace by bezeling the larger components using regular peyote stitch, then connects them with freeform beading. In these process photos Janice has yet to add fringe to the sand dollars' bezels. Her design is a careful balance of warm and cool tones with warm coral reds and cooler turquoise blues.

Facing Page: Sea Delight necklace by Janice Cuozzo.

Right and below: process photos of Sea Delight necklace by Janice Cuozzo. Compare these process photos to her finished piece to see the final touches still to come.

All photography on pages 128-132 by Valerie Hildebrand.

Sea Delight necklace by Janice Cuozzo. Inspired by a monthly bead challenge.
Photography by Valerie Hildebrand.

It is easier to see the freeform peyote connections in these two views of the back side of Janice's *Sea Delight* necklace.

Rather than using an Ultrasuede backing, her peyote stitch bezels leave the backs open. This technique is particularly useful for transparent cabochons such as crystals, and for decorative stones or other cabochons where the back may be as beautiful as the front.

To complete the necklace, Janice added a simple peyote stitch strap to both sides with a beaded loop and toggle closure.

Midnight Elegance Necklace

Midnight Elegance began with Janice's simple desire to make a black necklace for her sister-in-law. She knew she wanted to add several bezeled pieces, and that the foundation color would be black. This was enough for her intuitive design sense and working process. She chose various onyx beads, pearls, crystals, and seed beads in shades of black, gray and silver to compliment the jet and black diamond crystals of the bezeled components. She bezeled the crystals using regular peyote stitch with Delicas, size 15° seed beads and Charlottes. In keeping with her them of "elegance," Janice added some extra embellishment to the bezeled pieces after the necklace was fully constructed.

For her *Midnight Elegance* necklace, Janice stitched a length-wise section of regular peyote stitch seven rows wide, then used it as a base for freeform embellishment. In the photo at right, she is just past the necklace's halfway point, working right to left.

Five large, bezeled crystals form the central focal point, connected by freeform peyote bridges and layers of fringe and strung accent beads.

The second photo is a close-up of Janice's beaded bezels trailing beading thread. Janice uses the leftover beading thread from constructing her beaded bezels to stitch the components into the necklace.

She then further embellished the bezels as shown below in a close-up look at the underside of her necklace. Once again, it's easier to see the peyote stitch from this view.

Facing page: Janice Cuozzo's Midnight Elegance necklace.

This page: three closeups of Janice Cuozzo's construction process for her Midnight Elegance necklace.

All photos taken by Valerie Hildebrand.

Design Gallery

ADDITIONAL WORKS IN FREEFORM PEYOTE

Elven Blue Bracelet

by Liz Hart

Liz's *Elven Blue* bracelet proves that less can sometimes be more. Her open, curving lines and elegantly understated color scheme helped create a piece that would look perfect on the set of *Lord of the Rings*.

Inspired in part by the *Light and Dark* brooch from my first book on freeform peyote; Liz says it showed her that freeform peyote could be light and airy, yet also structurally sound. Taking that inspiration, Liz reinterpreted it in an entirely new direction. The beaded button clasp is Liz's original design.

Aphrodite,
Born of the Sea
by Bobbie Rafferty

Aphrodite started with the ceramic face. The piece grew and grew, until Bobbie ran out of steam to continue working on it. Then it lived on her work table for a long, long time. Long enough that it lived in two different states still unfinished. Bobbie packed it up when her family moved to their new home. Six years passed before she picked it back up again. Worth the wait, Aphrodite was accepted to be part of a juried exhibition called "About Face" at the Kentucky Artisans' Center in 2012.

Photography by Larry Berman.

First Holy Communion Veil

by Mary Foyes

Mary may have begun a family legacy with this gorgeous veil; made for her daughter's First Holy Communion.

Mary stitched each section from top to bottom, working along the width. Larger pearls and pressed glass connect the sections and create 'peek throughs', giving the band an open, lacy feel.

First Holy Communion Veil by Mary Foyes.
Photography by Shauna Landau Ploeger, Photography Du Jour. Modeled by Alicia Foyes.

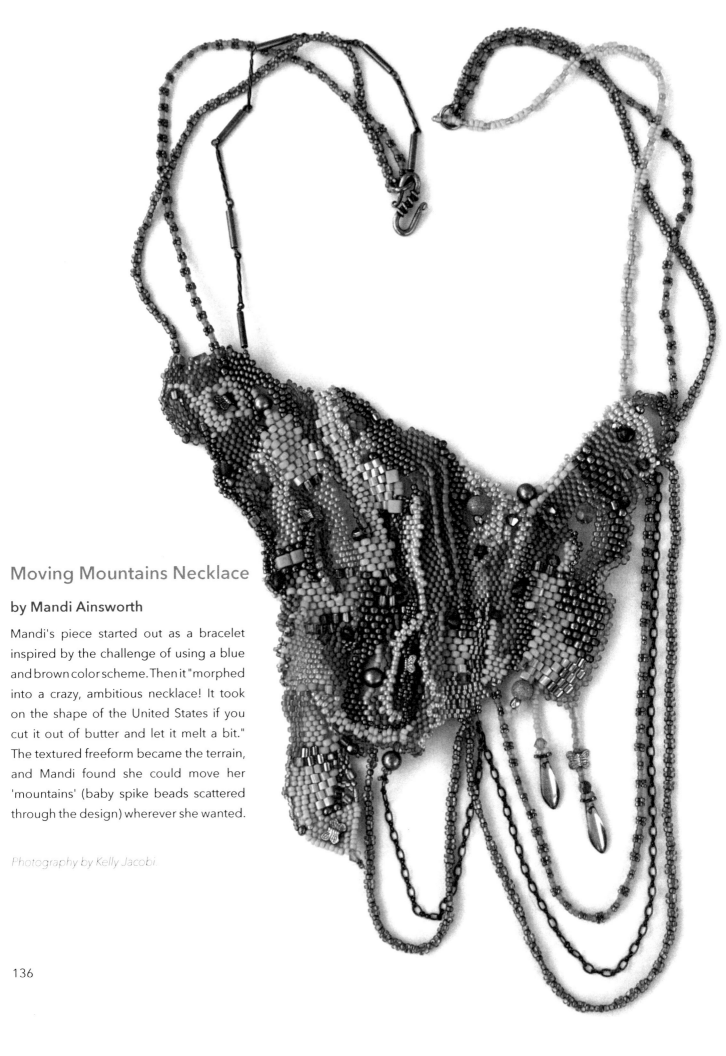

Moving Mountains Necklace

by Mandi Ainsworth

Mandi's piece started out as a bracelet inspired by the challenge of using a blue and brown color scheme. Then it "morphed into a crazy, ambitious necklace! It took on the shape of the United States if you cut it out of butter and let it melt a bit." The textured freeform became the terrain, and Mandi found she could move her 'mountains' (baby spike beads scattered through the design) wherever she wanted.

Photography by Kelly Jacobi.

CHAPTER FIVE

Beyond Jewelry

Beaded Forms & Freeform Sculpture

Beaded Forms

Beading over a form is one of the easiest way to create freeform sculptural pieces as the form provides a strong base of support for your bead weaving. Glass bottles of all shapes and sizes work particularly well in this capacity. They are relatively inexpensive, readily available, and come in an astonishing array of sizes and colors.

But don't limit yourself to bottles in your search for potential forms. Instead, choose a form that compliments the theme of your piece. Almost any shape can be beaded, some are simply more challenging than others. Paper maché forms, found objects, tree branches; I've even considered using a wooden egg - the only real limit is your imagination. In this chapter we will touch upon a few of the possibilities.

Fountain of Youth Beaded Bottle

Up until a few years ago, I believed glass bottles of Coca-Cola® were only a memory from my early childhood, before they were replaced by the ubiquitous aluminum can. Then, while studying at the Penland School of Craft in North Carolina, I came across these miniature bottles, standing about eight inches high. One of the staff members there had a penchant for them, and offered to give me her empties.

An iconic part of our culture, I couldn't stop musing about everything the brand and its bottles represent. While sitting at the laundromat, I sketched several ideas for a series of beaded bottles.

Unsure if I'd be able to find the little bottles back home, I ended up shipping an empty six-pack home, complete with its cardboard carrier. The bottles have sat on a shelf in my studio ever since, waiting for me to get started. To date, I've completed two of the six bottles in the series, with a third in process.

This is the first in that series. The *Fountain of Youth* - isn't that what the Coca-Cola® company promises? If we drink their carbonated soft drink, we'll always be young and cool and hip, full of energy?

For this piece, I decided to go with a mythical interpretation - Ponce de León meets Coca Cola®. Hence my vine-covered vessel commemorating the explorer's legendary search for the mythical well.

Working in Sections

I started with a base of cubic right angle weave in the round and three side panels of freeform peyote, each loosely shaped to fit the bottle's contours. I left space between the panels to allow room for creative license when stitching them into place around the bottle.

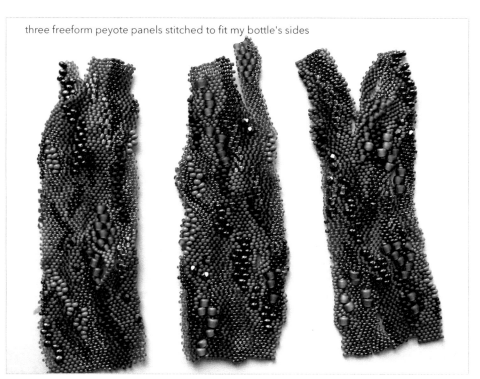

three freeform peyote panels stitched to fit my bottle's sides

Combining the Sections

It is easier to stitch freeform peyote flat, rather than around your form. For this reason, I recommend beading as much as possible in flat sections which can be stitched together later to fit your form.

Stitching each of the three panels to my beaded base, I left gaps between them. At this point, my beading reminded me of a banana peel wrapped around the bottle. The photo at left shows me testing the fit using twine to temporarily hold everything in place.

From here, it was simply a matter of working up the seams between panels. In some areas I stitched up along one side, narrowing the gap. Elsewhere, I created bridges crossing from one side to the other, then worked peyote stitch off of these bridges. My goal was to create a dense shell of greenery - like a deep forest or jungle seen from a distance.

Wanting to leave the top open, I faced the challenge of how to finish the bottle's lip. I stitched a tube of circular peyote stitch one inch tall which fit down inside the bottle. I was then able to use the tube's upper edge as anchors for my freeform beading.

I debated stopping here (the process photo at far right on following page), but decided to continue because the piece didn't scream 'jungle' yet to me.

Building the Vine Armatures

Next came the vines. After some experimentation, I created wire armatures in order to shape the vines way I wanted. Paper-wrapped wire painted a light green formed the central stem, with 18 gauge copper for the branches. I found it worked best to construct the complete armature before beginning to stitch. When I attempted to add branches after I finished the main stem, the copper wire had a tendency to poke through my beading.

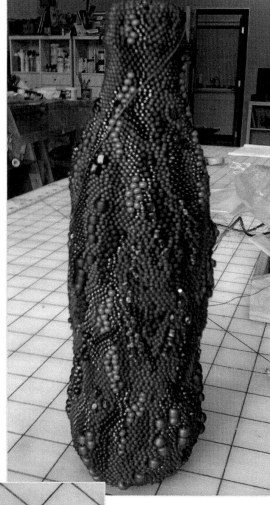

I built three separate vines, each similar to the one shown below. Working from the bottom, I started with size 11°s, then tapered to size 15°s for the top of the stem and the side branches.

I finished the central stem of each vine before beginning stitching the side branches.

Leaves and Flowers

All of the leaves and flowers were stitched separately. I added the leaves to the vines before draping and stitching the vines around the bottle. But I held off adding the flowers until the vines were secure. I wanted complete control over their placement to make sure that the flowers all faced outwards toward the viewer.

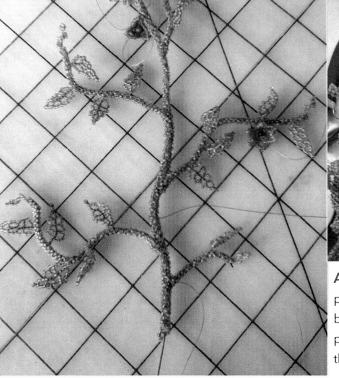

Above: determining the placement for several flower blossoms. Note the trailing pink threads leftover from their construction.

141

Message in a Bottle

What if there were a community of castaways, all of whom wished to send a message to the outside world? And what if between them, they possessed a single, seaworthy bottle? A solitary glass Coke® bottle (I'm overlooking the likely abundance of plastic water bottles in this vision).

Would they fight over whose message went into the bottle? Would they write one 'official' message from their entire community? Or might they stuff the bottle full of individual messages; a veritable cornucopia of hopes, dreams and wishes?

In my vision, it's the latter, with messages written on all manners of paper - receipts, post-it notes, fortune-cookie fortunes - whatever they had on hand. Thrown into the ocean, how long might that bottle drift before finally coming to rest on a distant shore?

Like that imaginary community of castaways, my bottle is filled with notes. Mine were gathered from my community of friends and fellow beaders. Some poignant, some quotations, many whimsical or pithy words of advice, they all wait hidden inside the heavy encrustation of beaded barnacles and coral.

Building Sea Creatures

Before starting in on the bottle itself, I had a lot of fun building 'sea critters' - beaded barnacles, nudibranches and anemones - to name a few. It was much easier to make these ahead of time, then stitch them into place as I built the bottle's beaded sheath.

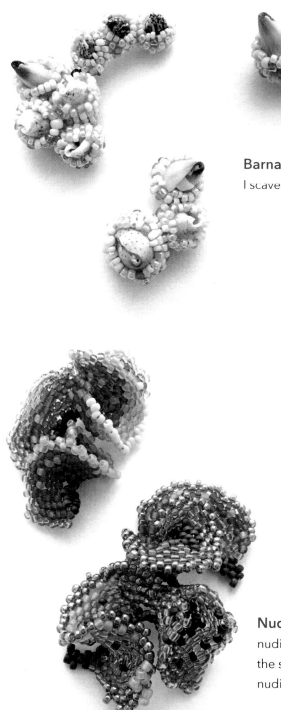

Barnacles - interconnected beaded bezels with real sea shells. I scavenged the smaller shells from seashell leis.

Anemones - I built these around 'gum drop' glass beads. Starting with a base of flat circular peyote using 11°s, I attached the gum drop bead then built a short wall the height of the bead, finishing the top edge with two rings of beaded fringe using 15°s.

Nudibranches - also known as sea slugs, I think nudibranches are some of the coolest forms under the sea! Here I used freeform ruffles to create several nudibranches, each between 2½ - 3½ inches long.

1) I built a base disc of cubic right angle weave in the round.

2) Starting to work freeform peyote off of the base. I alternated working on and off the bottle, checking the fit regularly to make sure my beading curved with the bottle.

3) My tension was tight enough for my stitching to support itself so long as it was just composed of seed beads.

4) Building beaded bezels for three sea shells. I later added extra bead work across the tops of two of the shells to hold them more securely and blend the beading into the whole.

144

Working on the Bottle

Left: The anemones add enough weight that the beading can no longer support itself. From this point, I had to tie it onto the bottle to check the fit.

I've added a largish shell to fill the lower circle. Taking advantage of the shell's flanges, I used as few bead bridges as possible so that the majority of the shell remains visible.

Unlike my previous beaded bottle, I found that I need to do most of the assembly work around the bottle itself. The weight of my beaded encrustations made it more difficult to work off the bottle as they tended to collapse and distort the overall shape of the beading.

Right: I've stitched the three bezeled shells into the main body of my bead work. When I wrapped the bezeled area around the bottle, two of the shells popped out of their bezels. While I was able to pop the shells back into place, the curvature of the bottle put a lot of pressure on their bezels. Worried that they weren't completely secure and might pop out again, I made a mental note to improve their bezels before I was done with the piece.

I also added one of my 'nudibranch' ruffles towards the base of the bottle by connecting the two ends of the ruffle into existing bead work.

Top view, looking down into the stitching. I placed two layers of acrylic felt inside my beaded base to cushion both my beading and the bottle.

Sea Glass. I bezeled the sea glass separately with right angle weave, then added it to the main body of beading.

Adding the barnacles. The bottle is upside down as it was easier to add the barnacles stitching from that direction.

Gum drop beads and stone chip encrustations add texture.

Improved bezels for the shells. More barnacles and anemones inch their way up the bottle.

I added my last two anemones. My focus was making sure the base beading curved snugly around the bottle. I filled the bottle with messages and sealed the top with a cork.

Covering the cork. I stitched a circular cap of freeform peyote, then stitched down to meld it into the sides.

An alternate view of the finished bottle.

148

Beaded Bottles by Cortney Phillips

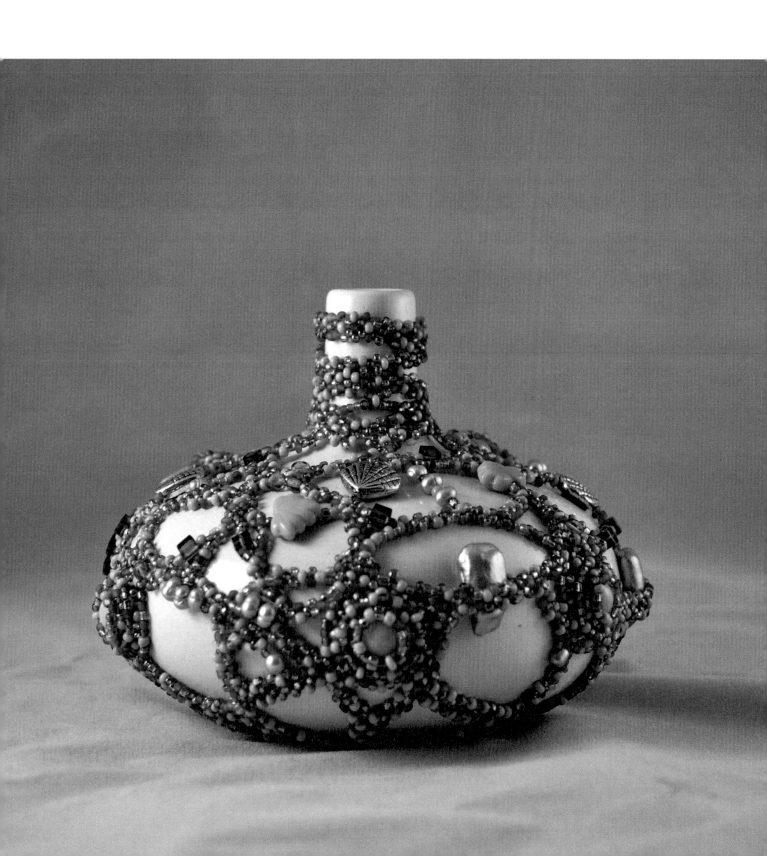

Beaded Bottles by Cortney Phillips

Druantia by Cortney Phillips

Creating the face from polymer clay, Cortney surrounded it with bead embroidery, then glued it to the bottle using 'copious amounts' of E6000 before surrounding it with freeform peyote. The antique bottle with its crooked top was the perfect backdrop for her design.

Cortney named her piece after Druantia, a mythical Gaelic goddess of fertility of both plants and animals. The name, Druantia is thought to come from the Celtic word for oak.

Untitled Bottle, previous page

Cortney began her blue beaded bottle by cutting a piece of suede to fit its bottom with an extra 3mm margin. Whip stitching beads around the edge of the suede, she glued the piece in place under the bottle. She also bead embroidered several 9mm cabochons, then glued them onto the bottle's sides as extra anchor points.

Worrying that the curvature of the bottle would present a challenge, Cortney began her bead weaving around the top and continued downward in a diagonal direction. She hoped that the beads would adhere to the slope of the bottle, which they did. The bottle itself was a photography prop she'd purchased years ago from a thrift store. The beads were leftovers from other projects and a seed bead mix she'd purchased when she first started beading. This bottle took Cortney five days to complete, while Druantia, her first bottle, took two weeks.

Previous page: Untitled Bottle (4" x 6") by Cortney Phillips.
Above: Druantia by Cortney Phillips. All photography by artist.

Nancy Dale

FEATURED ARTIST

Nancy Dale, bead artist and instructor extraordinare, shares a complete tutorial on creating freeform beaded rocks. The process is very similar to creating freeform beaded beads and could be adapted to cover other objects as well.

Froggie Knoll Freeform Peyote Covered Rock
Original Freeform Tutorial by Nancy Dale

There are many ways to approach wrapping an object with freeform stitching, but this is my normal path for wrapping up rocks. Rocks are wonderful as you can find them in any shape or size, and embellish them in any possible way; I prefer little forest or outdoor scenes, but of course you could make your rock into anything; a space ship, or the base of an ornament, or an abstract art object of any kind. I like to use mine purely for decoration, but you can also make good use of them as paperweights.

Beads and Supplies

Make a cup or so of bead soup - more or less depending on the size of your rock. I use 11°s, 15°s, 8°s, 6°s, and all manner of shaped seed beads (tiny cubes, hex beads, triangles, etc.), 2mm - 12mm accent beads and crystals, and my main focal bead (when I decide to use one - you don't have to!).

I always include some of my really 'good' beads in my soups, because I love the sparkle of Swarovski crystal, and can't ever resist freshwater pearls or a semi precious gemstone or two. I like to choose rocks that are rounded on the edges so that they won't break beads or cut my thread.

I recommend that you use a rock that fits comfortably in your hand and isn't very heavy, so that you won't get hand cramps while working. I use Fireline thread, but you can use any thread that makes you happy.

Finished photos of Froggie Knoll, freeform beaded rock (facing page and top right) by Sherwood Dale.

All process photos on pages 152-156 by Nancy Dale.

Wrapping the Rock in Freeform Peyote

1) To begin wrapping your rock, string a stop bead, and then a number of beads (odd or even, it doesn't matter) that will comfortably wrap around the widest part of your rock. It can overlap a tiny bit when you wrap it around the rock - when you add your next rows of work, it will shrink a bit. Hold your thread around the rock to check that it fits well. Once you have the right length, you're ready to start peyote stitch.

I like to work four to five rows of peyote stitch off of the beginning strand of beads before I anchor it to my rock. Check your length by measuring it around the rock a few times as you add rows.

Starting Row - should fit loosely around your rock.

2) Once you have worked a few rows, go ahead and wrap the work around your rock again, and join the ends together. It's OK if the band is still a bit loose - you can work three or four more rows with decreases if needed, to snug your band up to the rock so that it stays in place.

Protecting the Underside of your Beading

If you plan to use your rock as a paperweight or move it around regularly, you may want to cover the bottom of your rock with ultra suede or such rather than wrapping the bead work completely around; the beads underneath your rock may shatter if it's set down too hard, which in turn can lead to cut threads.

Simply cut out a piece of fabric the same size as the bottom of your rock, and work a brick stitch/picot edging all around the cut edge. Then proceed to work your freeform off of the edging and up around your rock.

Middle photo and lower right: Four rows of stitching - flat & wrapped around the rock.

3) String strands of beads from random places from one side of your band and around to the other side, to make a webbing that holds your band right where you want it to be. Add strands between those you just placed if it still looks as if your rock could escape the web. These can be slightly loose, as they will tighten as you work with them.

4) Now work freeform peyote along each of the strands of beads you placed, until each strand has snugged up to the rock.

Work about three rows on each strand before moving on to the next strand.

5) Once your rock is trapped happily in the beads, you can begin working in any direction you like. This is a good point to start adding in accent beads, as they make wonderful additions at the junction points between your band and your strands.

If you add a crystal diagonally at the square join, it makes for a much more pleasing transition of angles.

6) I like to work in circles counterclockwise along each of my 'empty' spaces until my rock is completely encased. You could work back and forth along each line, or in any direction that suits you. Adding more and more webbing would also be an option, for a really layered look. If you love the color of your rock, or have used a special piece of semi-precious stone as a base, you could stop here and leave your rock partially uncovered, as well.

Working in Circles, Filling Gaps

Filling the circle (1 of 3).

Filling the circle (3 of 3), and adding an accent bead.

accent bead from photo 3

Adding the frog bead on the opposite end from photo 3.

Filling the circle (2 of 3).

Adding the Focal Bead

I add my focal bead right near the end of my stitching, because it gives me a chance to choose which side is my 'up' side, and right where I want it to anchor into the base bead work. My frog bead has a hole that runs through his body parallel with the surface, so I used beads strung between two points to anchor him down - and passed back and forth through it many times before proceeding to weave around him. You could also wait until your rock was completely encased with beads, and then add your focal to the surface of your beading in the same way, or with a stop stitch (reinforced many times) if your bead hole runs top to bottom rather than across.

If your focal has a very small connection point - such as a mushroom bead - you might want to embroider your focal to a small piece of beading foundation so that it has a really sturdy base to work from. Edge the foundation as you would for any bead embroidery, but omit the backing fabric. Use a tiny amount of glue on the center ONLY of the back of the bead-worked piece to adhere your embroidery to the rock where you'd like it to sit, and work your freeform out from the edging once the glue is fully dried.

Make sure that your glue does not spread to the edge beads of your embroidered piece, or you may not be able to pass through those beads.

Once you have your focal securely in place, and have completed as much base beading as you like, you can add surface embellishments, bridges and ruffles, or anything that looks good to you. I left Froggie Knoll unembellished because I really enjoyed the look of the base beads, but on previous rocks I have added in ruffles, extra pearls and crystals on top, Lucite flower/leaf beads, and even bead woven flowers!

Julie's Rock

Another of Nancy's wonderful beaded rocks. Here, she added Lucite flowers and leaves to the miniature 'garden'. If you look closely, you can see the two rows of bead embroidery Nancy used around the base of the little mushroom house to help secure it to the base.

Right: 'Julie's Rock' by Nancy Dale. Photography by Sherwood Dale.

Seahorse Sculpture by Beth McGowan

Beth McGowan created her *Seahorse Sculpture* from a length of gnarled root (not driftwood, though it has that look). After covering several sections in peyote stitch, Beth stitched a series of freeform peyote ribbons stretching along the length of her piece, like seaweed draped across a submerged log.

The inset at right shows a detail of Beth's piece from the back, giving a closer look at her freeform peyote.

Freestanding Sculpture and Armatures

So far, we've looked at sculptures constructed over preexisting forms. But what if there is no preexisting form for the shape you wish to create?

For many smaller shapes, like the freeform fish that follow, peyote stitch has enough body to support the form without any internal structure. In these hollow forms, tension is the key. Keep your tension as tight as possible while beading and your beads will act as tiny building blocks. Kate McKinnon's *Contemporary Geometric Beadwork* is a great example of this, though not freeform.

For other shapes, you may wish to build your own structures or armatures to support your beading, as I did for my vines in my *Fountain of Youth* beaded bottle. A trip to the hardware or art supply store can yield many potential solutions, including wire, wire mesh, paper maché and more. When selecting materials, consider how it will wear and age over time as well as its immediate suitability. Will the wire you chose rust, corrode or oxidize? If yes, how might that affect your finished piece? For some themes of a particularly ecological or organic nature, the corrosion might be appropriate, but for most projects it is more likely to be problematic at best.

Georgia McMillan

FEATURED ARTIST

Georgia's Fish

Georgia's fish evolved from a regular peyote stitch beaded bead pattern she found in an issue of Bead & Button magazine. One of the sample beaded beads reminded Georgia of a little fish.

New to peyote stitch, Georgia wondered 'what if' and decided to give it a go. Because of her dyslexia, she often had trouble following counted patterns, instead teaching herself to follow her own instincts once she understood the basic stitch.

Starting in on her fish, she allowed the patterns to emerge as they wished. This wonderful series of fanciful fish was the result.

Fish Tips: Constructing the Body

Start with a Ring: Georgia begins each of her fish as a loop of beads equal to the size she wants for the largest part of the body. This is the center line for the body.

Peyote Stitch along one edge of your starting ring. She suggests stitching from the starting ring towards the head of your fish. That way, if it doesn't turn out as you hoped, then you can turn it into your tail and try again for a shapely head with the other half of the fish. Thus giving you two chances to get the shape of the head "right".

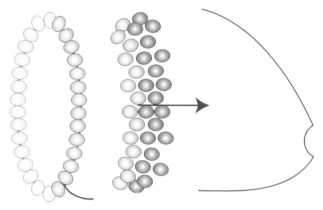

Starting loop of beads. Work off of one edge of your starting loop heading towards the future head of your fish.

Use decreases to shape the fish as you work. It's helpful to designate a "top" and "bottom" edge of your starting circle immediately (using different colors can make this easier). Make most of your decreases to either side of the top or bottom if you want to create a tapered oval fish body.

Change bead colors and shapes as you stitch. Think of your beads as fish scales and have fun playing with color and texture.

Think about the shape of the mouth before you get there. Do you want a wide, gaping mouth like the wonderful fish at right, or a pointed snout like the pink fish on the following page? Or would you prefer something in between? Use decreases to create the shape you desire, but be open to serendipity as well.

Left: close-up looks at one of Georgie's freeform fish from three angles.

Adding Character: Eyes & Mouths

Take a look at Georgia's eyes and mouths and how they add character to the wonderful facial expressions of each fish. For the eyes, she uses a variety of decorative beads, including flowers, discs, small buttons and coral discs.

Tip: You may want to add the eyes before you stitch the second half of the fish. They are a little easier to add when you can still reach inside the fish as you stitch. However, once added, they can snag your beading thread while you work. If you decide to wait to add the eyes, you may find it easier to use a curved beading needle.

Side Fins & Tails

The tails and fins are a great place to play with different fringing techniques and shaped beads. You don't need a lot of any one type, so it's also a great way to use up leftover beads from other projects.

In her fish, Georgia uses regular seed beads, bugles, daggers, drop beads and more.

Georgia's Fish Jewelry

While her fish make beautiful stand-alone sculptures, Georgia often incorporates them into her jewelry designs, such as the three examples shown here, include a brooch, pendant and a pair of goldfish earrings.

Above left: Fish brooch

Above right: the fish's top fin forms a bail for a simple, finger-knotted cord necklace.

Left: two gold fish earrings rest happily on the half shell.

Karen's Parrotish Fish

Anyone who knows me, knows fish are sort of my thing. I haven't kept a pet fish since my Beta, Mordred, died while I was in college, but I love stitching beaded fish friends. So it made perfect sense to use Georgia's general stitching techniques to create my own take on a freeform beaded fish.   The perfect no-maintenance pet!

Before selecting my beads, I drew a few quick sketches to get a feel for the fish I might like to create. Using markers, I drew several quick outlines, coloring them in with watercolor washes. I didn't bother worrying about tails or fins quite yet.   My first sketch was too cartoony. I based the next two loosely off of several Caribbean fish, including the Parrot Fish. I wasn't trying to make any particular type fish however, My concern here was just trying to try out different body shapes and the play of colors.

quick sketches with markers and watercolors

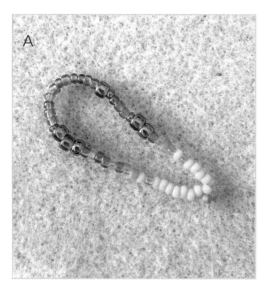

Starting the Body

Left: My starting ring with a stop bead. The opaque lime green beads marked my fish's future belly. To form my fish, I will need to work with a flattened ring, rather than a perfectly round tube.

Right: The same ring at six rows of peyote stitch. To this point, I have simply built upon the blocks of color from my starting row.

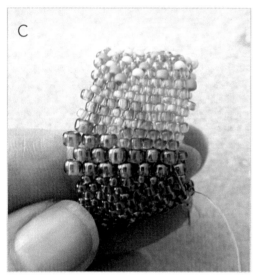

Tapering the Body

Left: I'm starting to decrease down towards what I hope will be my fish's head (remember Georgia's two chances). The ring is upside down in this picture.

Right: A look into the hollow ring as I stitch. I am placing most of my decreases along the bottom of the fish, inside the green bands because I want the belly of the fish to taper more than the top line.

Shaping the mouth

Left: Continuing to taper. Nearing the head, I took additional decreases in the middle of the fish to pull my beading in faster.

Right: It's a little crooked on one side. I think this adds a little extra character, so I did not try to fix it. As you can see, I decided to go with a wide open mouth.

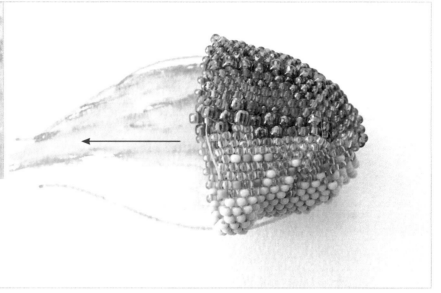

Returning to the middle line, I began stitching towards the back of the fish.

Right: Comparing my beading to my sketch, I was surprised how closely I'd followed the outline.

where I want to stop stitching the body

Left: Continuing to shape the body as I stitch.

Above: Taking a decrease at the center bottom, worked over three rows to create a gentler taper.

Left: Shaping the tail as a tall, narrow oval. I want to end the body right where it tapers to the narrowest point, to leave room to attach the tail to the body with later stitching.

Right: Zipping the two sides of the body together in preparation for adding the tail fins.

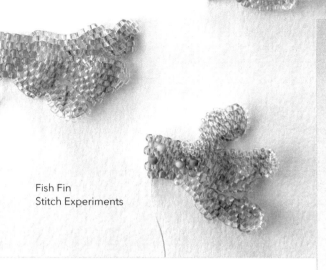

A

Fish Fin
Stitch Experiments

sketching fins on tracing paper

It was time for fins. The question was what did I want them to look like? Going back to my sketchbook, I grabbed a sheet of tracing paper and played with several options, trying them on my fish bodies rather like you might change clothing on a paper doll.

I thought I liked the fins at the far right best, so I started stitching and ended up with the fin at the top left above (A). It matches the side fin I envisioned perfectly, and absolutely did not work on my fish! So I tried again, resulting in the sample at top right. I liked this better, but it was too geometric.

The lower two fins had a far more organic feel. I also liked how the light blue thread gave an 'underwater' quality to the transparent beads.

starting row 8 beads wide

11° seed beads

15° seed beads

Building the Tail Fin

Left: I started with a short ribbon of peyote stitch 8 beads wide, matching colors from the fish body before flaring into the tail with size 15's.

Right: Building one section of the tail at a time, I made sure to include interesting voids between tail petals. All of the beads past the 'body' are 15° transparents.

building the next section

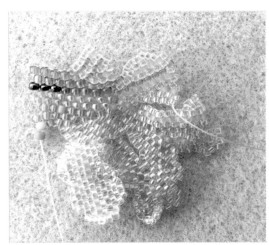

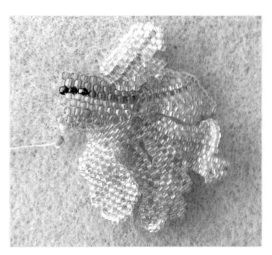

Left: Working toward the top, I'm using the idea of sea fans to help me create the tail.

Right: The tail is finished, now it's time to attach it to the body. Note that I left my original stop bead in place.

Preparing to attach the tail: I decided that the body section of the tail was too long, so I took out two rows before using peyote stitch to zip the tail onto the body.

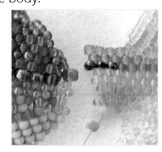

attaching the eyes using a curved needle

For the eye, I used a 6mm cat's eye bead, then surrounded it with two layers of beading - the first 11°s, the second with 15°s. Last, I attached both side fins into the green area of the body using the left over thread from their creation.

Featured Artist Biographies

Jennifer Porter, a member of the Northwest Bead Society, draws her inspiration from the unlikliest places during her walks and kayaking adventures around her home in the Pacific Northwest. When asked about her creative process, she replied "My creative process is based on the fact that I cannot follow a recipe. I *have* to make things unique."

Natalia Malysheva learned to sew and knit from her mother in early childhood; her love for needlework in its many variants has continued throughout her life. Natalia started to play with beads in 2009 and discovered freeform beading two years later. She describes freeform bead weaving as a 'limitless field: it is possible to play with colors, textures, sizes and forms. So the freeform beading is a meditation; it gives me energy and satisfaction."

Natalia doesn't see herself as an artist, but sees her work as simply something she has to do. "I think that everyone wants to be able to make something themselves. Because everyone needs the beauty, the confidence, to feel like someone who can create, not only consume."

For more of Natalia's work visit her Facebook page, Aqvatali-Jewelry, her blog http://aqvatali.blogspot.com and her Etsy shop www.etsy.com/shop/Aqvatali.

Cynthia Machata's work is eclectic and bohemian, heavily influenced by her travels and the history of the places she visits. She writes a regular blog and often includes the stories about the people and places who become the inspiration behind her jewelry. While new to freeform beading, she's embraced the style and has found freedom in bead weaving by being to relax some of the rules. It has opened up a new world of creativity and pattern design in her work. You'll also find her regularly contributing on Creative Bead Chat's Facebook group and is the lead editor behind the magazine.

For more of Cynthia's work, visit antiquitytravelers.blogspot.com and www.etsy.com/shop/AntiquityTravelers.

Wendy Hatton first started using beads in around 2000 while working on an art series based on the life and times of the Ancient Egyptians.

Fortunate enough to own her own store where she sold beads gathered from around, this led her into designing, writing and kitting her own tutorials as well as conducting workshops in many cities and towns in Australia. Wendy also wrote for the publishers of an Australian Beading magazine, "Beads Etc". In 2006 she won the Inaugural Beads Etc and Stitches and Craft Australian Jewelry Designer of The Year Award. This took her on an amazing journey around the world where she was able to study some of the world's best examples of beaded jewelry.

Wendy finds the design process to be the truly great thing about beading. In her words, "working freeform gives me total license to let the beads and design evolve and take on a shape of it's own. The beads have a very free spirit which we try to contain. I like to just let them work their own 'magic'."

Janice Cuozzo, a native of Boston, relocated to the sunny southwest town of Cave Creek, AZ. Shortly after her journey to the Wild West she joined a group of fellow artists participating in monthly bead challenges. These challenges helped her work evolve and expanded her range of techniques. Janice developed a reputation for creating jewelry that incorporated many cabochons with seed bead bezels and lots of bead fringe. Upon discovering freeform peyote, she quickly made it her own, adding her bezeled elements and fringe. One of her first pieces using this technique was selected as a finalist in the 2014 Bead Dreams competition.

Asked what drew her to freeform bead weaving, Janice replied "I am an artist by nature and an engineer by design. I started working with seed beads in 2012 and was instantly hooked on the variety of possibilities. I look at nature for my inspiration. Colors, shapes and textures are my favorite elements to use in my designs. Playing with bead shapes, sizes and colors are essential in the initial design phase. Before my discovery of freeform peyote, I had a much more structured approach where I drew many sketches before starting to stitch. Freeform peyote allows me the freedom to execute designs with extreme fluidity and vigor. My designs are intricate and still very well structured but the openness of the free form peyote technique has added a new level of whimsy and fantasy to my jewelry creations. Happiness for me is intricacy in a well thought out design."

See more of Janice's work at www.facebook.com/janicecuozzoartist.

Nancy Dale has been beading for over 25 years, and is mainly focused on off-loom weaving techniques. She loves freeform peyote (or any freeform beading) for the meditative quality it brings, and for the freedom it offers for creative self expression. She finds the non-linear nature of it allows the mind to truly rest and wander, and frequently allows for more creativity becoming available for other, more structured design work. Her necklace, "Dryad" made it into the finals of Bead Dreams 2009. Nancy lives in Vermont with her husband and her three dogs and her work has been published in various beading books and magazines.

For more of Nancy's work visit www.nedbeads.com or her blog at http://nedbeads.com/NEDbeads/Blog.html. Her original bead weaving patterns are available on her Etsy site www.etsy.com/shop/nedbeads.

Georgia McMillan was born in Snohomish, Washington, where she studied lapidary in high school. After her marriage to a fellow rock hound, she studied silver smithing under the tutelage of Lulu Robertson, before making her career as a silversmith for the next twenty five years.

Introduced to bead weaving by her adult daughters, Georgia fell in love with the possibilities and the portability of working with seed beads. Dyslexia made following traditional patterns difficult, leading her to develop her own instead. Inspired by a magazine article on peyote stitched beaded beads, she challenged the members of the Seedbeaders' group she'd founded to create their own versions. As Georgia worked on her entry, the form taking shape reminded her of a fish and she decided to take that idea and run with it.

Karen Williams, artist, author and workshop instructor, Karen has spent the past ten years exploring the medium of freeform bead weaving. Drawn to the medium by the colors and textures of the beads and their limitless potential; she is never happier than to spend the day with beads and a needle, waiting to see what might appear. As much as she she enjoys bead weaving, Karen loves teaching because it gives her a chance to see what others might do with the same techniques.

Explorations in Freeform Peyote Beading is her third book on bead weaving, and her second on freeform peyote. She has taught workshops throughout the country and regularly teaches in the Seattle area, where she makes her home.

Online, she maintains an active blog, baublicious.blogspot.com, Facebook page www.facebook.com/skunkhillstudio, and founded the Freeform Peyote Group on Facebook.

Additional Works by

Mandi Ainsworth

www.beadcircle.com

Ibolya Barkóczi

www.etsy.com/shop/ibics

Sherry Eagle of eaglewomyn designs

eaglewomyn@yahoo.com

Marlene Oman Emmons

emmons45241@yahoo.com

Mary Foyes of Veils by M

www.facebook.com/VeilsByM or veilsbym@comcast.net

Liz Hart

www.facebook.com/TreetopBeadworks or treetopbeadworks@tx.rr.com

Lisa Jones

moxie_beads@yahoo.com

Mary Kearney

www.facebook.com/GarnishesJewelry

Ellen Lambright of Jewelry By Ellen

www.ellensjewelry.com or ellenl@ellensjewelry.com

Sarah Meadows

www.saturdaysequins.com

Beth McGowen of Kitobird Studio

kitobirdstudio.com or bmcgowan@kitobirdstudio.com

Marsha Melone

Cortney Phillips

www.facebook.com/BaublesbyCortney

Bobbie Rafferty of Beadsong Jewelry

beadsong.blogspot.com or beadsong@aol.com

Index

Frilly pendant by Liz Hart.

*Freeform peyote beads by Lisa Jones.
Photography by artist.*

Resources & References

Fire Mountain Gems

1.800.423.2319
www.firemountaingems.com

Fusion Beads

online store, also classes in store in Seattle
13024 Stone Ave N, Seattle, WA 98133
1.888.781.3559 or 206.781.9500
www.fusionbeads.com

Shipwreck Beads

8560 Commerce Place Dr., Lacey, WA 98516
1.800.950.4232
www.shipwreckbeads.com

Znet Shows

sea glass, Chinese crystals & glass pearls
www.znetshows.com

Ocean Sky Beads

www.oceanskybeads.com

Books & Blogs

My Social Media pages

(these are pages run by author, Karen Williams)
my blog: baublicious.blogspot.com
www.facebook.com/skunkhillstudio
www.facebook.com/freeformpeyotebeading

Freeform Peyote Facebook Group

www.facebook.com/groups/freeformpeyote/

Contemporary Geometric Beadwork

by Kate McKinnon
beadmobile.wordpress.com/

Sally Russick's new blog

(mentioned in conjunction with my *Rattlesnake Choker*)
http://sallyrussick.blogspot.com/

Independent Artists

D. Lynne Bowland - Islandgirl

enameled poppies & head pins (and lampworked beads)
store: www.etsy.com/shop/islandgirl
website: www.fireballbeeds.com
blog: www.islandgirlsinsites.blogspot.com

Juli Cannon - Jules Beads

lampworked focals and bead sets
www.etsy.com/shop/StudioJuls

JJ Jacobs - Creative Soul Revival

lampworked and fused glass cabochons, beads and more
store: www.etsy.com/shop/CreativeSoulRevival
website: www.comingabstractions.com (this site is for her acrylic paintings - her contemporary, abstract designs makes JJ one of my favorite freeform artists working in another medium).

Debbie Sanders Glass (DSG Beads)

lampworked beads and discs
www.etsy.com/shop/debbiesanders

Trinket Foundry (Cathy Collison)

tumbled glass shapes and more
www.trinketfoundry.com

Fern Hill Glass

the source for glass 'cabochons' Cynthia Machata used in her *Surf* necklace
www.fernhillglass.com/

Made in United States
North Haven, CT
17 October 2021